Tav Is for Torah

Hebrew for Adults
Book 4

Linda Motzkin
The author of
Aleph Isn't Tough,
Aleph Isn't Enough, and
Bet Is for B'reishit

Hara Person, series editor

The author gratefully acknowledges the following for permission to reprint previously published material:

HANA AMICHAI: From *Shalvah Gedolah: She'elot U-Teshuvot* by Yehuda Amichai, copyright © 1980. Used by permission of Hana Amichai.

JEWISH PUBLICATION SOCIETY: Excerpts from *JPS Hebrew-English Tanakh: The Traditional Hebrew Text and the New JPS Translation,* Second Edition © 1999 by the Jewish Publication Society. Reprinted by permission of Jewish Publication Society.

KOREN PUBLISHERS JERUSALEM, LTD.: Excerpts from *The Jerusalem Bible* copyright © 1998 by Koren Publishers Jerusalem. Reprinted by permission of Koren Publishers Jerusalem, Ltd.

MESORAH PUBLICATIONS, LTD.: Reproduced from *The Chumash,* The Stone Edition, Artscroll Series, edited by Rabbi Nosson Scherman and Rabbi Meir Zlotowitz. Reprinted with permission from the copyright holders Artscroll / Mesorah Publications, Ltd.

SCHOCKEN BOOKS: From *The Five Books of Moses* by Everett Fox, copyright © 1983, 1986, 1990, 1995 by Schocken Books. Used by permission of Schocken Books, a division of Random House, Inc.

JEWISH LIGHTS: Excerpt from *God Was In This Place and I, i did not know* © 1994 Lawrence Kushner (Woodstock, VT: Jewish Lights Publishing).

A Note on the Translations

The translations provided in this book in the Additional Reading and Translation Practice sections are as close to literal as possible, so that you can easily compare them with the original language. In some instances, a word or phrase is followed by another possible translation that is included in brackets {like this}. A different style of brackets [like this] occasionally appears in this book and is used to indicate words not included in the Hebrew that have been inserted for clarity in the English translation.

Moreover, the terms יְיָ and יְהוָֹה can be translated in several different ways, as seen in the Torah text translations cited in each odd-numbered chapter. In our own translations, we have chosen to translate these terms as "Eternal One," "The Eternal One," "The Eternal." Likewise, in our own translations we have chosen to translate the Hebrew pronouns referring to God not as "He" or "Him" (nor "It" or "Its") but as "God" and "God's" followed by brackets {like this} indicating the literal masculine translation.

978-0-80740-847-6

Behrman House

Millburn, New Jersey

www.behrmanhouse.com

Manufactured in the United States of America

Acknowledgments

Tav Is for Torah is the fourth book in the URJ Hebrew for Adults Series. Along with the first three books, *Aleph Isn't Tough, Aleph Isn't Enough,* and *Bet is for B'reshit,* it owes its existence to the vision of Rabbi Eric Yoffie, President of the URJ, who inaugurated a historic campaign in 1996 to revive Hebrew literacy throughout the Reform movement. The (then) UAHC Hebrew Literacy Task Force, co-chaired by Rabbis Jan Katzew and Lawrence Raphael, was convened to respond to this challenge, and provided direction and input in the development of this series.

Many rabbis and educators in the field of Hebrew language instruction agreed to pilot this text in adult classes in their communities and provided valuable perspectives and suggestions regarding adult Hebrew learning. I am particularly grateful to David Blumberg for the extensive and detailed notes he provided from his piloting experience, and to Harriet Rosen who provided helpful "from-the-field" feedback.

I have been blessed with a wonderful community, Temple Sinai of Saratoga Springs, New York. I owe them much thanks for all their support and encouragement, and for the six-month sabbatical during which a portion of this book was written. I am also grateful to Congregation B'nei Israel in San Jose, Costa Rica and to the Monteverde Society of Friends in Monteverde, Costa Rica, for the way they welcomed and embraced my family during our sabbatical there.

I was privileged to teach two adult Hebrew classes this year at Temple Sinai. I am grateful to the students in my Hebrew II class for giving me the opportunity to share my enthusiasm for and love of the Hebrew language: Pat Freund, Cheryl Glick, Barbara Levine, Ruth Andrea Levinson, Evelyn Markowitz, Benita Pittinger, Mimi Rayl, Jerry Silverman, David Spingarn, and Wendy Zeh. And I am grateful to the students in Hebrew IV for sticking with their Hebrew studies long enough to develop their own love and appreciation for the nuances of the language, and for all their marvelous insights, questions, and creative *midrashim*: Lollie Abramson Stark, Cathy DeDe, Eleanor deVries, Diana Fenton, Dianna Goodwin, Carla Gordon, Cynthia Guile, Tina Marlowe, Deborah Meyers, Art Ruben, and Mark Steinberger.

At the URJ Press, there were a number of people who assisted in various steps toward the publication of this book. Rabbi Hara Person, Editor-in-Chief of the URJ Press, was the guiding light for each volume in this series. Her attention to detail, while never losing sight of the larger whole, is reflected on every page. It has been a pleasure to work with her at every stage of this process. Those who provided helpful assistance in all the various aspects of the production of this book include: Ken Gesser, Liane Broido, Joel Eglash, Debra Hirsch Corman, Lauren Dubin, Victor Ney, Ron Ghatan, and Debbie Fellman.

And finally, my thanks and appreciation go to my family: my three wonderful children, Rachel, Ari, and Shira, who are an ongoing source of delight and inspiration, and their father, my husband, co-rabbi, and life partner, Rabbi Jonathan Rubenstein, who has enriched my life in more ways than I could begin to recount. Their love and support are my life's greatest blessings.

Table of Contents

UNIT ONE

Chapter 1 1

Welcome
Torah Study Text: Genesis 28:10–17
Translating the Torah Study Text
Torah Translations
Vocabulary יֵשׁ יָם אָנֹכִי אֲנִי אֵלֶּה זֹאת זֶה
The Roots ל־ק־ח י־ר־א
Torah Commentary
Exercises
Extra Credit: The Patriarchs and Daily Prayer

Chapter 2 15

Torah Study Text: Vocabulary and Root Review
Building Blocks: זֶה and זֹאת and אֵלֶּה
This and That
Grammar Enrichment: ה Meaning "Toward"
Torah Study Text with Building Blocks
Additional Reading and Translation Practice
Exercises
From Our Texts: Mishnah Pe-ah 1:1

UNIT TWO

Chapter 3 28

Torah Study Text: Exodus 3:1–7
Translating the Torah Study Text
Torah Translations
Vocabulary כִּי תּוֹךְ אֵשׁ מִדְבָּר אַחַר כֹּהֵן
The Roots ב־ו־א ר־א־ה
Torah Commentary
Exercises
Extra Credit: Layers of Meaning in Torah Study

Chapter 4 41

Torah Study Text: Vocabulary and Root Review
Building Blocks: אֲנִי and אָנֹכִי Verb Forms
Perfect Forms: The תִּי Ending
Imperfect Forms: The א Prefix
The Endings ▒ִי and ▒ַי and נִי

Torah Study Text with Building Blocks
Grammar Enrichment: Perfect and Imperfect Forms
Additional Reading and Translation Practice
Exercises
From Our Texts: "Ani Maamin"

UNIT THREE

Chapter 5 **57**

Torah Study Text: Leviticus 19:1–4, 15–17, 33–34
Translating the Torah Study Text
Torah Translations
Vocabulary חֵטְא אֵל עֵדָה גֵּר מִשְׁפָּט לֵאמֹר
The Roots ע־מ־ד נ־שׂ־א
Torah Commentary
Exercises
Extra Credit: All the Rest is Commentary

Chapter 6 **71**

Torah Study Text: Vocabulary and Root Review
Building Blocks: "You" Verb Forms
Perfect Forms: The תָ and תֶם Endings
Imperfect Forms: The ת Prefix and וּ Ending
Torah Study Text with Building Blocks
Grammar Enrichment: Perfect and Imperfect Forms for אַתָּה and אַתֶּם
Additional Reading and Translation Practice
Exercises
From Our Texts: "Instead of a Love Poem"

UNIT FOUR

Chapter 7 **87**

Torah Study Text: Deuteronomy 5:6–7, 12–18
Translating the Torah Study Text
Torah Translations
Vocabulary לְמַעַן שַׁעַר בַּת מְלָאכָה כַּאֲשֶׁר אַחֵר
The Roots נ־ו־ח כ־ב־ד
Torah Commentary
Exercises
Extra Credit: The Fourth Commandment

Chapter 8 101

Torah Study Text: Vocabulary and Root Review
Building Blocks: "Have" and "Not Have" in Hebrew
"Have" and "Not Have" in the Perfect and Imperfect
Torah Study Text with Building Blocks
Grammar Enrichment: אֲשֶׁר
Additional Reading and Translation Practice
Exercises
From Our Texts: לְכָל אִישׁ יֵשׁ שֵׁם

UNIT FIVE

Chapter 9 114

Torah Study Text: Deuteronomy 30:11–16, 19
Translating the Torah Study Text
Torah Translations
Vocabulary רַע מָוֶת לִפְנֵי קָרוֹב הַיּוֹם
The Roots מ־ו־ת ע־ב־ר
Torah Commentary
Exercises
Extra Credit: Not in Heaven

Chapter 10 126

Torah Study Text: Vocabulary and Root Review
Building Blocks: אֲנַחְנוּ and אָנוּ Verb Forms
Perfect Forms: The נוּ Ending
Imperfect Forms: The נ Prefix
Torah Study Text with Building Blocks
Grammar Enrichment: Perfect and Imperfect Forms of אָנוּ and אֲנַחְנוּ
An Additional Note on Hebrew Verb Patterns
Additional Reading and Translation Practice
Exercises
From Our Texts: "Hava Nagila"
A Concluding Thought

Verb Charts 140

Glossary 151

Verb Review

Before beginning *Tav is for Torah*, you may find it helpful to review the verb forms that were introduced in *Aleph Isn't Enough* and *Bet is for B'reishit*. There are several different verb patterns in Hebrew, as explained in *Bet is for B'reishit* chapters 8 and 10, and three of them have been introduced in this series: פָּעַל **Pa'al**, פִּעֵל **Pi'el** and הִפְעִיל **Hif'il**.

Participle, perfect and imperfect verb forms were presented for each of these three verb patterns. These forms are reviewed in the charts below. The book and chapter in which they were introduced are indicated in parentheses.

Participles

Pa'al פָּעַל ***(A.I.E. Ch 4)***

f pl ■וֹ■ְ■וֹת *m pl* ■וֹ■ְ■ִים *f sg* ■וֹ■ֶ■ֶת *m sg* ■וֹ■ֵ■

Pi'el פִּעֵל ***(A.I.E. Ch 10, B.I.F.B. Ch 7)***

f pl מְ■ַ■ְּ■וֹת *m pl* מְ■ַ■ְּ■ִים *f sg* מְ■ַ■ֶּ■ֶת *m sg* מְ■ַ■ֵּר

Hif'il הִפְעִיל ***(B.I.F.B. Ch 10)***

f pl מַ■ְ■ִי■וֹת *m pl* מַ■ְ■ִי■ִים *f sg* מַ■ְ■ִי■ָה *m sg* מַ■ְ■ִי■

Certain root letters cause variations in these participle forms. Sometimes the vowels change or a root letter may disappear. The participle forms for all the roots introduced in this series are provided in the verb charts in the back of this book.

Perfect Verbs

Pa'al פָּעַל

3rd person pl ■ָ■ְ■וּ (B.I.F.B. Ch 6) *3rd person f sg* (הִיא) ■ָ■ְ■ָה (B.I.F.B. Ch 4) *3rd person m sg* (הוּא) ■ָ■ַ■ (B.I.F.B. Ch 2)

Pi'el פִּעֵל ***(B.I.F.B. Ch 8)***

3rd person pl ■ִ■ְּ■וּ *3rd person f sg* (הִיא) ■ִ■ְּ■ָה *3rd person m sg* (הוּא) ■ִ■ֵּ■

Hif'il הִפְעִיל ***(B.I.F.B. Ch 10)***

3rd person f sg (הִיא) הִ■ְ■ִי■ָה *3rd person m sg* (הוּא) הִ■ְ■ִי■

3rd person pl הִ■ְ■ִי■וּ

Certain root letters cause variations in these forms. Sometimes the vowels change or a root letter may disappear. Such changes can also occur when a reversing vav is attached. The perfect forms for all the roots introduced in this series are provided in the verb charts in the back of this book.

Imperfect Verbs

Pa'al פָּעַל

When the פָּעַל Pa'al imperfect forms were introduced in *Bet is for B'reishit*, no vowels were provided. This is because almost none of the verb roots presented in this series follow the regular vowel pattern listed below. All of the verb roots, except ז־כ־ר, מ־ל־ך and ש־מ־ר, have some sort of variation in the vowels of the imperfect forms, caused by certain root letters.

3rd person m sg (הוּא) יִ■ְ■ֹ■ (*B.I.F.B. Ch 2*)

3rd person f sg (הִיא) תִּ■ְ■ֹ■ (*B.I.F.B. Ch 4*)

3rd person pl יִ■ְ■ְ■וּ (*B.I.F.B. Ch 6*)

Pi'el פִּעֵל *(B.I.F.B. Ch 8)*

3rd person m sg (הוּא) יְ■ַ■ֵּ■

3rd person f sg (הִיא) תְּ■ַ■ֵּ■

3rd person pl יְ■ַ■ְּ■וּ

Hif'il הִפְעִיל *(B.I.F.B. Ch 10)*

3rd person m sg (הוּא) יַ■ְ■ִי■

3rd person f sg (הִיא) תַּ■ְ■ִי■

3rd person pl יַ■ְ■ִי■וּ

Certain root letters cause variations in these forms. Sometimes the vowels change or a root letter may disappear. Such changes can also occur when a reversing vav is attached. The imperfect forms for all the roots introduced in this series are provided in the verb charts in the back of this book.

Welcome — בְּרוּכִים הַבָּאִים

Tav Is for Torah is the final volume in the URJ Hebrew curriculum for adults. It is organized in the same way as *Bet Is for B'reishit*, with five units consisting of two chapters each, integrating the learning of classical Hebrew with a guided study of selected Torah passages. In this book, you will study text selections from four of the five books of the Torah. May you be spiritually enriched by your continued study of Torah in Hebrew!

Torah Study Text: Genesis 28:10–17

Jacob, the grandson of Abraham and Sarah and the son of Isaac and Rebekah, must leave his parental home and travel to unfamiliar terrain. In our selection below, as he begins his journey, he dreams of a ladder (or stairway) to heaven and receives assurance that God will be with him wherever he goes.

This passage contains many words, Hebrew roots, and grammatical concepts that have not yet been introduced. You are not expected to be able to read this entire passage. Read the Hebrew below to see how many of the words you can recognize. Underline or circle the words, roots, endings, and prefixes that you know.

10 וַיֵּצֵא יַעֲקֹב מִבְּאֵר שָׁבַע וַיֵּלֶךְ חָרָנָה׃ 11 וַיִּפְגַּע בַּמָּקוֹם וַיָּלֶן שָׁם
כִּי־בָא הַשֶּׁמֶשׁ וַיִּקַּח מֵאַבְנֵי הַמָּקוֹם וַיָּשֶׂם מְרַאֲשֹׁתָיו וַיִּשְׁכַּב
בַּמָּקוֹם הַהוּא׃ 12 וַיַּחֲלֹם וְהִנֵּה סֻלָּם מֻצָּב אַרְצָה וְרֹאשׁוֹ מַגִּיעַ
הַשָּׁמָיְמָה וְהִנֵּה מַלְאֲכֵי אֱלֹהִים עֹלִים וְיֹרְדִים בּוֹ׃ 13 וְהִנֵּה יְהוָה
נִצָּב עָלָיו וַיֹּאמַר אֲנִי יְהוָה אֱלֹהֵי אַבְרָהָם אָבִיךָ וֵאלֹהֵי יִצְחָק
הָאָרֶץ אֲשֶׁר אַתָּה שֹׁכֵב עָלֶיהָ לְךָ אֶתְּנֶנָּה וּלְזַרְעֶךָ׃ 14 וְהָיָה זַרְעֲךָ
כַּעֲפַר הָאָרֶץ וּפָרַצְתָּ יָמָּה וָקֵדְמָה וְצָפֹנָה וָנֶגְבָּה וְנִבְרְכוּ בְךָ
כָּל־מִשְׁפְּחֹת הָאֲדָמָה וּבְזַרְעֶךָ׃ 15 וְהִנֵּה אָנֹכִי עִמָּךְ וּשְׁמַרְתִּיךָ בְּכֹל
אֲשֶׁר־תֵּלֵךְ וַהֲשִׁבֹתִיךָ אֶל־הָאֲדָמָה הַזֹּאת כִּי לֹא אֶעֱזָבְךָ עַד
אֲשֶׁר אִם־עָשִׂיתִי אֵת אֲשֶׁר־דִּבַּרְתִּי לָךְ׃ 16 וַיִּיקַץ יַעֲקֹב מִשְּׁנָתוֹ

וַיֹּאמֶר אָכֵן יֵשׁ יְהוָה בַּמָּקוֹם הַזֶּה וְאָנֹכִי לֹא יָדָעְתִּי׃ 17 וַיִּירָא וַיֹּאמַר
מַה־נּוֹרָא הַמָּקוֹם הַזֶּה אֵין זֶה כִּי אִם־בֵּית אֱלֹהִים וְזֶה שַׁעַר
הַשָּׁמָיִם׃

Translating the Torah Study Text

The Torah Study Text, Genesis 28:10–17, is reprinted below. Underneath each Hebrew word is a literal translation (except for the word אֶת, which has no English translation). This literal translation of the individual words does not produce a smooth English reading of the passage. In order to arrange the words into meaningful English sentences, it is necessary to draw upon your knowledge of the building blocks of the Hebrew language. It is also necessary to make choices between various possible translations of individual words and phrases.

Using your knowledge of the building blocks of the Hebrew language and the meanings of the words provided below, translate this passage into clear English sentences. Write your translation on the lines following the text. This selection includes some grammatical forms and vocabulary that have not yet been introduced. You will need to rely, in part, on the translations provided.

Genesis 28:10–17

חָרָנָה׃	וַיֵּלֶךְ	שָׁבַע	מִבְּאֵר	יַעֲקֹב	וַיֵּצֵא
toward Haran	*and he went/ walked*	*Beer-sheba*	*from*	*Jacob*	*and went out*

הַשֶּׁמֶשׁ	בָא	כִּי־	שָׁם	וַיָּלֶן	בַּמָּקוֹם	וַיִּפְגַּע
the sun	*had come in/set*	*because*	*there*	*and spent the night*	*the place*	*and he encountered*

וַיִּשְׁכַּב	מְרַאֲשֹׁתָיו	וַיָּשֶׂם	הַמָּקוֹם	מֵאַבְנֵי	וַיִּקַּח
and he lay down	*[at/under] his head place*	*and he put*	*the place*	*from stones (of)*	*and he took*

וְרֹאשׁוֹ	אַרְצָה	מֻצָּב	סֻלָּם	וְהִנֵּה	וַיַּחֲלֹם	בַּמָּקוֹם הַהוּא׃
and its top	*earthward*	*set up*	*ladder/ stairway*	*and behold/ here*	*and he dreamt*	*in that place*

מַגִּיעַ	הַשָּׁמָיְמָה	וְהִנֵּה	מַלְאֲכֵי	אֱלֹהִים
reaching	*heavenward/ toward the heavens*	*and behold/ here*	*angels/ messengers (of)*	*God*

עֹלִים	וְיֹרְדִים	בּוֹ:	וְהִנֵּה	יְהוָה	נִצָּב	עָלָיו
ascending	*and descending*	*on it*	*and behold/ here*	*the Eternal*	*standing*	*on/over/it/him*

וַיֹּאמַר	אֲנִי	יְהוָה	אֱלֹהֵי	אַבְרָהָם	אָבִיךָ	וֵאלֹהֵי	יִצְחָק
and he said	*I*	*the Eternal*	*God (of)*	*Abraham*	*your father*	*and God (of)*	*Isaac*

הָאָרֶץ	אֲשֶׁר	אַתָּה	שֹׁכֵב	עָלֶיהָ	לְךָ	אֶתְּנֶנָּה	וּלְזַרְעֶךָ:
the land/ ground	*that*	*you*	*lying*	*on it*	*to you*	*I will give it*	*and to your seed/offspring*

וְהָיָה	זַרְעֲךָ	כַּעֲפַר	הָאָרֶץ	וּפָרַצְתָּ
and will be	*your seed/ offspring*	*like dust*	*the earth*	*and you will spread out*

יָמָּה	וָקֵדְמָה	וְצָפֹנָה	וָנֶגְבָּה
toward the sea (westward)	*and eastward*	*and northward*	*and toward the Negev (southward)*

וְנִבְרְכוּ	בְךָ	כָּל־	מִשְׁפְּחֹת	הָאֲדָמָה
and they shall be blessed/bless themselves	*in you*	*all*	*families (of)*	*the earth*

וּבְזַרְעֶךָ:	וְהִנֵּה	אָנֹכִי	עִמָּךְ	וּשְׁמַרְתִּיךָ	בְּכֹל
and in your seed/ offspring	and behold/ here	I	with you	and I will guard/ keep you	in all

אֲשֶׁר־	תֵּלֵךְ	וַהֲשִׁבֹתִיךָ	אֶל־	הָאֲדָמָה הַזֹּאת	כִּי	לֹא
that	you may/ will go	and I will bring you back	to	this land	for	not

אֶעֱזָבְךָ	עַד	אֲשֶׁר	אִם־עָשִׂיתִי	אֵת אֲשֶׁר־	דִּבַּרְתִּי	לָךְ:
I will leave you	until	that	I have done	that which	I have spoken	to you

וַיִּיקַץ	יַעֲקֹב	מִשְּׁנָתוֹ	וַיֹּאמֶר	אָכֵן	יֵשׁ	יְהוָה	בַּמָּקוֹם הַזֶּה
and he awoke	Jacob	from his sleep	and he said	surely	there is	the Eternal	in this place

וְאָנֹכִי	לֹא	יָדָעְתִּי:	וַיִּירָא	וַיֹּאמַר	מַה־	נּוֹרָא
and I	not	I knew	and he was afraid/ awestruck	and he said	how	awesome/ fearsome

הַמָּקוֹם הַזֶּה	אֵין זֶה	כִּי אִם־	בֵּית	אֱלֹהִים	וְזֶה	שַׁעַר
this place	this is not/none	but	house (of)	God	and this	gate (of)

הַשָּׁמָיִם:
the heaven

TORAH Translations

Translation from one language to another is not an exact science but a subjective art. Every translation is an interpretation of the original text, as there are often several possible ways that a given verse, or even a single word, can be understood. The following translations of our Torah Study Text: Genesis 28:10–17 all take slightly different approaches to the text. Compare your translation above with these Torah translations. Notice the subtle differences between each of these translations and your own.

10 Jacob left Beer-sheba, and set out for Haran. 11 He came upon a certain place and
stopped there for the night, for the sun had set. Taking one of the stones of that place,
he put it under his head and lay down in that place. 12 He had a dream; a stairway was
set on the ground and its top reached to the sky, and angels of God were going up and
down on it. 13 And the LORD was standing beside him and He said, "I am the LORD, the
God of your father Abraham and the God of Isaac: the ground on which you are lying I
will assign to you and to your offspring. 14 Your descendants shall be as the dust of the
earth; you shall spread out to the west and to the east, to the north and to the south.
All the families of the earth shall bless themselves by you and your descendants.
15 Remember, I am with you: I will protect you wherever you go and will bring you back
to this land. I will not leave you until I have done what I have promised you."
16 Jacob awoke from his sleep and said, "Surely the LORD is present in this place, and
I did not know it!" 17 Shaken, he said, "How awesome is this place! This is none other
than the abode of God, and that is the gateway to heaven."

JPS HEBREW-ENGLISH TANAKH: THE TRADITIONAL HEBREW TEXT AND THE NEW JPS TRANSLATION—2D ED. PHILADELPHIA: JEWISH PUBLICATION SOCIETY, 1999.

10 Jacob departed from Beer-sheba, and went toward Haran. 11 He encountered the place
and spent the night there because the sun had set; he took from the stones of the place
which he arranged around his head, and lay down in that place. 12 And he dreamt, and
behold! A ladder was set earthward and its top reached heavenward; and behold!
angels of God were ascending and descending on it.
13 And behold! HASHEM was standing over him, and He said, "I am HASHEM, God of
Abraham your father and God of Isaac; the ground upon which you are lying, to you
will I give it and to your descendants. 14 Your offspring shall be as the dust of the earth,
and you shall spread out powerfully westward, eastward, northward and southward;
and all the families of the earth shall bless themselves by you and by your offspring.
15 Behold, I am with you; I will guard you wherever you go, and I will return you to this
soil; for I will not forsake you until I will have done what I have spoken about to you."
16 Jacob awoke from his sleep and said, "Surely HASHEM is present in this place and I

did not know!" [17]*And he became frightened and said, "How awesome is this place! This is none other than the abode of God and this is the gate of the heavens!"*

THE CHUMASH, ARTSCROLL SERIES, STONE EDITION. BROOKLYN: MESORAH PUBLICATIONS, 1993.

10Yaakov went out from Be'er-Sheva, and went toward Harran,
11and encountered a certain place.
He had to spend the night there, for the sun had come in.
Now he took one of the stones of the place
and set it at his head
and lay down in that place.
12And he dreamt:
Here, a ladder was set up on the earth,
its top reaching the heavens,
and here: messengers of God were going up and down on it.
13And here:
YHWH was standing over against him.
He said:
I am YHWH,
the God of Avraham your father and the God of Yitzhak.
The land on which you lie
I give to you and to your seed.
14Your seed will be like the dust of the earth;
you will burst forth, to the Sea, to the east, to the north, to the Negev.
All the clans of the soil will find blessing through you and through your seed!
15Here, I am with you,
I will watch over you wherever you go
and will bring you back to this soil;
indeed, I will not leave you
until I have done what I have spoken to you.
16Yaakov awoke from his sleep
and said:
Why,
YHWH is in this place,
and I, I did not know it!
17He was awestruck and said:
How awe-inspiring is this place!

This is none other than a house of God,
and that is the gate of heaven!

THE FIVE BOOKS OF MOSES: A NEW TRANSLATION WITH INTRODUCTIONS, COMMENTARY, AND NOTES BY EVERETT FOX. NEW YORK: SCHOCKEN BOOKS, 1995.

And Ya'aqov went out from Be'er-sheva, and went toward Haran. And he lighted on a certain place, and tarried there all night, because the sun was set; and he took of the stones of that place, and put them under his head, and lay down in that place to sleep. And he dreamed, and behold a ladder set up on the earth, and the top of it reached to heaven: and behold the angels of GOD ascending and descending on it. And, behold, the LORD stood above it, and said, I am the LORD GOD of Abraham thy father, and the GOD of Yizhaq: the land on which thou liest, to thee will I give it, and to thy seed; and thy seed shall be as the dust of the earth, and thou shalt spread abroad to the west, and to the east, and to the north, and to the south: and in thee and in thy seed shall all the families of the earth be blessed. And, behold, I am with thee, and will keep thee in all places to which thou goest, and will bring thee back to this land; for I will not leave thee, until I have done that which I have spoken to thee of. And Ya'aqov awoke out of his sleep, and he said, Surely the LORD is in this place; and I knew it not. And he was afraid, and said, How dreadful is this place! this is no other than the house of GOD, and this is the gate of heaven.

THE JERUSALEM BIBLE, PUBLISHED FOR THE NAHUM ZEEV WILLIAMS FAMILY FOUNDATION AT HECHAL SHLOMO, JERUSALEM. JERUSALEM: KOREN PUBLISHERS JERUSALEM LTD., 1969.

Vocabulary

The word אֵלֶּה does not appear in the Torah Study Text: Genesis 28:10–17. Locate the rest of the vocabulary words in the text.

this *m*	—	זֶה
this *f*	—	זֹאת
these	—	אֵלֶּה
I	—	אֲנִי
I	—	אָנֹכִי
sea *m*	—	יָם
there is, there are	—	יֵשׁ

Notes on the Vocabulary

1. The words אֲנִי and אָנֹכִי both mean "I" and are used for masculine and feminine subjects. אֲנִי has become the common word for "I" in modern Hebrew.
2. The word יֵשׁ can mean "being," "substance," or "existence." More often, however, its usage is like the opposite of the word אֵין, introduced in Chapter 7 of *Aleph Isn't Enough.*

The root י־ר־א connotes both "fear" and "awe" or "reverence." This root follows the פָּעַל verb pattern, with some irregularities. The participle, perfect, and imperfect forms can be found in the verb charts in the back of the book.

In this chapter's Torah Study Text, the root י־ר־א appears twice in verse 17. The root letter י drops out in the word נוֹרָא.

(verse 17)

(and) he was afraid/awestruck and he said	—	וַיִּירָא וַיֹּאמַר

(verse 17)

how awesome/fearsome is this place	—	מַה־נּוֹרָא הַמָּקוֹם הַזֶּה

The following words and expressions, both ancient and modern, are derived from the root י־ר־א. The first root letter י drops out in some words formed from this root.

fearing, apprehensive, revering, venerating	—	יָרֵא
God-fearing, pious, reverent	—	יְרֵא אֱלֹהִים
fear, terror, awe	—	יִרְאָה
piety, religiousness {fear/terror/awe of heaven}	—	יִרְאַת שָׁמַיִם
fear, reverence	—	מוֹרָא
fearsome, awesome (*in modern Hebrew:* awful, awfully, very much)	—	נוֹרָא
amazing things	—	נוֹרָאוֹת
the High Holy Days {awe-inspiring/awesome days}	—	יָמִים נוֹרָאִים

THE ROOT ל-ק-ח

The basic meaning of the root ל-ק-ח is "take." This root follows the פָּעַל verb pattern, with some irregularities. The participle, perfect, and imperfect forms can be found in the verb charts in the back of the book.

The root ל-ק-ח appears once in our Torah Study Text. The first root letter ל has dropped out:

(verse 11)

and he took from the stones of the place	—	וַיִּקַּח מֵאַבְנֵי הַמָּקוֹם

The following words, both ancient and modern, are derived from the root ל-ק-ח. The first root letter ל drops out in some words formed from this root.

learning, teaching	—	לֶקַח
pilferer, petty thief	—	לַקְחָן
booty, prey, loot	—	מַלְקוֹחַ
jaws *(poetic)*	—	מַלְקוֹחַיִם
tongs, fire tongs, snuffers, pincers	—	מֶלְקָחַיִם
pliers	—	מֶלְקַחַת
taking, receiving, buying	—	מִקָּח
merchandise, goods	—	מַקָּחָה

TORAH Commentary

Much of Torah commentary arises from the fact that Hebrew words and phrases can be understood in more than one way. Often a commentary stems from a detail in the Hebrew text that may be lost or obscured in an English translation. Preceding each of the following selections, the Hebrew detail giving rise to the commentary is explained.

The phrase at the beginning of verse 11, וַיִּפְגַּע בַּמָּקוֹם, "and he encountered the place," can be understood in different ways. The verb וַיִּפְגַּע has a range of meanings: "he encountered, hit, struck" and even "he entreated, prayed." The word הַמָּקוֹם can mean both "the place" and, in rabbinic literature, "God, the Omnipresent, the One who is in all places."

Dramatic, unexpected encounter happens here, in space and in time. "He collided with a certain place"—the word va-yifga *suggests a dynamic encounter with an object that is traveling toward oneself. The force of the meeting is palpable but mysterious.*

Traditionally, the "certain place" is identified with Mount Moriah, "where Jacob's father was bound in sacrifice." This is the future place of the Holy Temple, of prayer and sacrifice, of the human attempt to come close to God. It is a place of purity and danger, of great longing and strict distancing. But the makom, *the "certain place," is equally a metaphoric reference to God Himself, "who is the Place of the universe, while the universe is not His place." Jacob, therefore, makes contact here with God Himself.*

AVIVAH GOTTLIEB ZORNBERG, *GENESIS: THE BEGINNING OF DESIRE.* PHILADELPHIA: JEWISH PUBLICATION SOCIETY, 1995.

The sequence of the verbs עֹלִים וְיֹרְדִים, "ascending and descending," in verse 12 has given rise to much commentary. Lawrence Kushner summarizes some of the traditional rabbinic interpretations and provides an additional, contemporary insight.

A careful reading of the text reveals that the "angels were going up and coming down" on the ladder. The sequence is wrong. If angels reside in heaven, shouldn't the order be the opposite, coming down and going back up? Rabbinic tradition offers several possible explanations.

One suggests that, since Jacob was about to leave the land of Israel, one group of angelic escorts was returning to Heaven and another was descending to watch over him as he began his travels abroad. Another possibility is that the angels symbolized the nations of the world, whose power ascends and descends during the course of history. And still a different interpretation proposes that the angels were not ascending and descending the ladder but were exalting and degrading Jacob, going up and down, as it were, "on him."

But there is another, even more obvious interpretation. The angels did not reside in heaven at all. They lived on earth. They were ordinary human beings. And, like ordinary human beings, they shuttled back and forth between heaven and earth. The trick is to remember, after you descend, what you understood when you were high on the ladder.

LAWRENCE KUSHNER, *GOD WAS IN THIS PLACE & I, I DID NOT KNOW.* WOODSTOCK, VT.: JEWISH LIGHTS PUBLISHING, 1993.

The word עָלָיו in verse 13 is ambiguous. It could refer to either the ladder or Jacob.

וְהִנֵּה יְהוָֹה נִצָּב עָלָיו, ***And behold, the Eternal stood on/over it/him.*** *Rabbi Chiya and Rabbi Yanai disagree. One holds that* עָלָיו *means "on the ladder" while the other says that* עָלָיו *means "over Jacob." The view that* עָלָיו *means "on the ladder" presents no difficulty; regarding the view that it refers to Jacob, it means that God stood [protectively] over him.*

B'REISHIT RABBAH 69:3

At the end of verse 17, Jacob proclaims וְזֶה שַׁעַר הַשָּׁמָיִם, "and this is the gate of heaven." Jacob's statement might imply that this is the only point of access to the heavenly realm. But the Chasidic rabbi, Menachem Mendl of Kotzk, teaches that there are many gates to God.

> ***This is the gate of heaven...****One can reach God anywhere. The difference is which gate one uses to approach Him. If one goes through the gate of heaven, one finds Him immediately. But if one uses other gates, one also finds other things along the way.*
>
> R. Menachem Mendl of Kotzk, as quoted in *Torah Gems*, comp. Aharon Yaakov Greenberg, trans. R. Dr. Shmuel Himelstein. Tel Aviv and Brooklyn: Yavneh Publishing House, Chemed Books, 1998.

Exercises

1. Make flash cards for each of the new vocabulary words and Hebrew roots introduced in this chapter, or use the flash card set published as a companion to this book. Review the cards to learn all of them.

2. Draw a line connecting each Hebrew word to its English translation. For some words, there can be more than one correct translation.

there are	זֹאת
this	אֲנִי
sea	יָם
I	יֵשׁ
these	זֶה
there is	אֵלֶּה
	אָנֹכִי

3. On the left are plural forms of words introduced as vocabulary in this chapter. Draw a line connecting each plural word to its singular form or forms. Translate both into English.

________________	אֲנַחְנוּ	זֶה	________________
		זֹאת	________________
________________	אֵלֶּה	יָם	________________
		אֲנִי	________________
________________	יַמִּים	אָנֹכִי	________________

4. Read and translate the following groups of words.

a.
- הַיָּם הַגָּדוֹל ________________
- רוּחַ הַיָּם ________________
- מֵי הַיָּם ________________
- מִיָּם עַד יָם ________________
- יָם מִצְרַיִם ________________

b.
- אֲנִי בִּנְךָ ________________
- אֲנִי אֱלֹהֵיכֶם ________________
- אֲנִי הַמֶּלֶךְ ________________
- זֶה הַמֶּלֶךְ ________________
- זֹאת הַתּוֹרָה ________________

c.
- זֶה הַיָּם ________________
- זֶה הָעָם ________________
- זֶה הַמָּקוֹם ________________
- זֶה הַנָּבִיא ________________
- זֶה הַמַּלְאָךְ ________________

d.
- כָּל זֹאת ________________
- כָּל אֵלֶּה ________________
- מִי אֵלֶּה? ________________
- מִי זֹאת? ________________
- זֹאת הָאִשָּׁה ________________

e.
- יֵשׁ אֱלֹהִים ________________
- יֵשׁ רוֹפֵא ________________
- יֵשׁ רְפוּאָה ________________
- יֵשׁ רַחֲמִים ________________
- יֵשׁ דֶּרֶךְ ________________

f.
- מִי אָנֹכִי? ________________
- נַעַר אָנֹכִי ________________
- אָנֹכִי עִמָּכֶם ________________
- אָנֹכִי אֱלֹהֵי אָבִיךָ ________________
- הֲשֹׁמֵר אָחִיךָ אָנֹכִי? ________________

5. Identify the root of each of the following verbs and whether it is a perfect, imperfect, or participle form. Translate.

Translation	**Form**	**Root**	**Verb**
			יִהְיֶה
			עָבַד
			יוֹשְׁבִים
			לוֹקְחִים
			לָקַח
			מְבָרֵךְ
			מַמְלִיךְ
			מוֹצִיא
			הָלְכָה
			יָרְאָה
			יוֹדְעוֹת
			תִּבְנֶה

Extra Credit: The Patriarchs and Daily Prayer

In the Jewish tradition, there are three set times for daily prayer services: שַׁחֲרִית, morning; מִנְחָה, afternoon; and מַעֲרִיב, evening. In the Talmud, *Berachot* 26b, two different explanations are offered for the establishment of these set times of prayer. One opinion, expressed in the name of Rabbi Yehoshua ben Levi, is that the prayers were instituted to replace the daily sacrifices (offered in the ancient Temple in Jerusalem before its destruction by the Romans in the year 70 C.E.). Another viewpoint, given in the name of Rabbi Yosei bar Chanina, is that the times of prayer were inaugurated by the three Patriarchs, Abraham, Isaac, and Jacob. According to this view, it was Abraham who began the practice of morning prayer. This is suggested by Genesis 19:27, where it says: וַיַּשְׁכֵּם אַבְרָהָם בַּבֹּקֶר אֶל־הַמָּקוֹם אֲשֶׁר־עָמַד שָׁם אֶת־פְּנֵי יְהוָֹה, "And Abraham got up early in the morning to the place [*or:* to the Omnipresent] where he stood there before [*or:* with the face of] the Eternal." Isaac began the practice of afternoon prayer, as implied in Genesis 24:63: וַיֵּצֵא יִצְחָק לָשׂוּחַ בַּשָּׂדֶה לִפְנוֹת עָרֶב, "And Isaac went out to meditate in the field before evening." Jacob, then, is the patriarch who began the practice of evening prayer, and the passage cited to support this view comes from this chapter's Torah Study Text, verse 11: וַיִּפְגַּע בַּמָּקוֹם. As noted in Avivah Zornberg's Torah commentary above, these words can be understood to mean both "he encountered the place" and "he prayed to/entreated the Omnipresent." The time of day indicated in this verse is בָא הַשֶּׁמֶשׁ, "the sun had set."

There is an additional Chasidic teaching derived from the notion that Jacob inaugurated the evening prayer at this particular point in his life journey, in a time of great personal stress, as he was fleeing alone from his home to a place unknown:

> *This is a hint to us that even if a person is at the lowest point and in darkness, he should not despair, but should gird whatever strength he has left and should pray. After all, here Jacob was in great distress and everything seemed to be dark around him. He nonetheless was not taken aback and was composed enough to pray.*

SHEM MI-SHMUEL, AS QUOTED IN *TORAH GEMS*, COMP. AHARON YAAKOV GREENBERG, TRANS. R. DR. SHMUEL HIMELSTEIN. TEL AVIV AND BROOKLYN: YAVNEH PUBLISHING HOUSE, CHEMED BOOKS, 1998.

Torah Study Text: Vocabulary and Root Review

This unit's Torah Study Text, Genesis 28:10–17, is reprinted below, highlighting the new vocabulary words as well as the words formed from the new Hebrew roots introduced in Chapter 1. Read this passage again, recalling the meaning of each of the highlighted words or roots.

10 וַיֵּצֵא יַעֲקֹב מִבְּאֵר שָׁבַע וַיֵּלֶךְ חָרָנָה׃ 11 וַיִּפְגַּע בַּמָּקוֹם וַיָּלֶן שָׁם
כִּי־בָא הַשֶּׁמֶשׁ **וַיִּקַּח** מֵאַבְנֵי הַמָּקוֹם וַיָּשֶׂם מְרַאֲשֹׁתָיו וַיִּשְׁכַּב
בַּמָּקוֹם הַהוּא׃ 12 וַיַּחֲלֹם וְהִנֵּה סֻלָּם מֻצָּב אַרְצָה וְרֹאשׁוֹ מַגִּיעַ
הַשָּׁמָיְמָה וְהִנֵּה מַלְאֲכֵי אֱלֹהִים עֹלִים וְיֹרְדִים בּוֹ׃ 13 וְהִנֵּה יְהוָה
נִצָּב עָלָיו וַיֹּאמַר **אֲנִי** יְהוָה אֱלֹהֵי אַבְרָהָם אָבִיךָ וֵאלֹהֵי יִצְחָק
הָאָרֶץ אֲשֶׁר אַתָּה שֹׁכֵב עָלֶיהָ לְךָ אֶתְּנֶנָּה וּלְזַרְעֶךָ׃ 14 וְהָיָה זַרְעֲךָ
כַּעֲפַר הָאָרֶץ וּפָרַצְתָּ **יָמָּה** וָקֵדְמָה וְצָפֹנָה וָנֶגְבָּה וְנִבְרְכוּ בְךָ
כָּל־מִשְׁפְּחֹת הָאֲדָמָה וּבְזַרְעֶךָ׃ 15 וְהִנֵּה **אָנֹכִי** עִמָּךְ וּשְׁמַרְתִּיךָ בְּכֹל
אֲשֶׁר־תֵּלֵךְ וַהֲשִׁבֹתִיךָ אֶל־הָאֲדָמָה **הַזֹּאת** כִּי לֹא אֶעֱזָבְךָ עַד
אֲשֶׁר אִם־עָשִׂיתִי אֵת אֲשֶׁר־דִּבַּרְתִּי לָךְ׃ 16 וַיִּיקַץ יַעֲקֹב מִשְּׁנָתוֹ
וַיֹּאמֶר אָכֵן **יֵשׁ** יְהוָה בַּמָּקוֹם **הַזֶּה** **וְאָנֹכִי** לֹא יָדָעְתִּי׃ 17 **וַיִּירָא**
וַיֹּאמַר מַה־**נּוֹרָא** הַמָּקוֹם **הַזֶּה** אֵין **זֶה** כִּי אִם־בֵּית אֱלֹהִים
וְזֶה שַׁעַר הַשָּׁמָיִם׃

Building Blocks

זֶה and זֹאת and אֵלֶּה

The Hebrew words זֶה and זֹאת both mean "this." זֶה is used for masculine subjects, and זֹאת is used for feminine subjects. Examples:

This is the place.	—	זֶה הַמָּקוֹם.	This is the man.	—	זֶה הָאִישׁ.
This is the Torah.	—	זֹאת הַתּוֹרָה.	This is the woman.	—	זֹאת הָאִשָּׁה.

The Hebrew word אֵלֶּה, meaning "these," is used with both masculine and feminine plural subjects.

These are the men/people.	—	אֵלֶּה הָאֲנָשִׁים.
These are the women.	—	אֵלֶּה הַנָּשִׁים.

In all the examples above, the word "is" or "are" is included in the English translation, forming a sentence. There is another usage of זֶה, זֹאת, and אֵלֶּה, in which the word "is" or "are" does not appear and only a phrase is formed. Compare the two different usages below. Notice that the word order is different and that the letter ה is attached to both the subject and to the word זֶה, זֹאת, or אֵלֶּה when forming a phrase.

this place	—	הַמָּקוֹם הַזֶּה	This is the place.	—	זֶה הַמָּקוֹם.
this woman	—	הָאִשָּׁה הַזֹּאת	This is the woman.	—	זֹאת הָאִשָּׁה.
these people	—	הָאֲנָשִׁים הָאֵלֶּה	These are the people.	—	אֵלֶּה הָאֲנָשִׁים.

Both types of usage appear in this chapter's Torah Study Text:

(verse 15)

and I will bring you back to this land	—	וַהֲשִׁבֹתִיךָ אֶל־הָאֲדָמָה הַזֹּאת

(verse 16)

surely there is the Eternal in this place	—	אָכֵן יֵשׁ יְהוָה בַּמָּקוֹם הַזֶּה

(verse 17)

how awesome/fearsome is this place	—	מַה־נּוֹרָא הַמָּקוֹם הַזֶּה

(verse 17)

there is none this but {this is none but} the house of God	—	אֵין זֶה כִּי אִם־בֵּית אֱלֹהִים

(verse 17)

and this is the gate of heaven	—	וְזֶה שַׁעַר הַשָּׁמָיִם

This and That

The English words "this" and "these" and the Hebrew words זֶה, זֹאת, and אֵלֶּה generally refer to something that is either physically near by or close in time. The English words "that" or "those" imply more distance in space or time. In Hebrew, the pronouns הוּא, "he," הִיא, "she," הֵם, "they" (masculine), and הֵן, "they" (feminine), can be used in place of זֶה, זֹאת, and אֵלֶּה to mean "that" and "those," implying more distance in space or time. Examples:

this time/season	—	הַזְּמַן הַזֶּה
that time/season	—	הַזְּמַן הַהוּא
these days	—	הַיָּמִים הָאֵלֶּה
those days	—	הַיָּמִים הָהֵם
this land	—	הָאָרֶץ הַזֹּאת
that land	—	הָאָרֶץ הַהִיא

A well-known example of these usages occurs in the second blessing said over the Chanukah candles:

בָּרוּךְ אַתָּה יְיָ אֱלֹהֵינוּ מֶלֶךְ הָעוֹלָם, שֶׁעָשָׂה נִסִּים לַאֲבוֹתֵינוּ

Blessed are You, Eternal our God, Sovereign of the universe, who did miracles for our ancestors

in those days	בַּיָּמִים הָהֵם
at this time/season.	בַּזְּמַן הַזֶּה.

In this chapter's Torah Study Text, the usage of הַהוּא appears once, at the end of verse 11:

and he lay down in that place	—	וַיִּשְׁכַּב בַּמָּקוֹם הַהוּא

GRAMMAR Enrichment

ה Meaning "Toward"

When the letter ה is attached to the end of a word, it can have the same meaning as the ending "ward" in English (e.g. homeward, westward), implying "to" or "toward." The following examples, all taken from this chapter's Torah Study Text, are provided for enrichment only. It is not necessary to memorize these words.

Haran-ward, toward Haran	—	חָרָנָה	←	Haran (name of a city)	—	חָרָן
earthward, toward earth	—	אַרְצָה	←	earth	—	אֶרֶץ
heavenward, toward the heavens	—	הַשָּׁמַיְמָה	←	the heavens	—	הַשָּׁמַיִם
seaward, toward the sea	—	יָמָּה	←	sea	—	יָם
eastward, toward the east	—	קֵדְמָה	←	east	—	קֶדֶם
northward, toward the north	—	צָפֹנָה	←	north	—	צָפוֹן
toward the Negev, southward	—	נֶגְבָּה	←	Negev (southern region of Israel)	—	נֶגֶב

Torah Study Text with Building Blocks

Following is this unit's Torah Study Text, Genesis 28:10–17, reprinted with both the new Building Blocks and Grammar Enrichment material highlighted. Reread this text, noting the different usages of זֶה, זֹאת, and הַהוּא, and the ה ending meaning "toward." A translation is provided below for only the highlighted Building Blocks. For a translation of the entire passage, refer back to Chapter 1.

[10] וַיֵּצֵא יַעֲקֹב מִבְּאֵר שָׁבַע וַיֵּלֶךְ **חָרָנָה**: [11] וַיִּפְגַּע בַּמָּקוֹם וַיָּלֶן שָׁם
כִּי־בָא הַשֶּׁמֶשׁ וַיִּקַּח מֵאַבְנֵי הַמָּקוֹם וַיָּשֶׂם מְרַאֲשֹׁתָיו וַיִּשְׁכַּב
בַּמָּקוֹם הַהוּא: [12] וַיַּחֲלֹם וְהִנֵּה סֻלָּם מֻצָּב **אַרְצָה** וְרֹאשׁוֹ מַגִּיעַ
הַשָּׁמָיְמָה וְהִנֵּה מַלְאֲכֵי אֱלֹהִים עֹלִים וְיֹרְדִים בּוֹ: [13] וְהִנֵּה יְהוָה
נִצָּב עָלָיו וַיֹּאמַר אֲנִי יְהוָה אֱלֹהֵי אַבְרָהָם אָבִיךָ וֵאלֹהֵי יִצְחָק

הָאָרֶץ אֲשֶׁר אַתָּה שֹׁכֵב עָלֶיהָ לְךָ אֶתְּנֶנָּה וּלְזַרְעֶךָ׃ 14 וְהָיָה זַרְעֲךָ
כַּעֲפַר הָאָרֶץ וּפָרַצְתָּ **יָמָּה וָקֵדְמָה וְצָפֹנָה וָנֶגְבָּה** וְנִבְרְכוּ בְךָ
כָּל־מִשְׁפְּחֹת הָאֲדָמָה וּבְזַרְעֶךָ׃ 15 וְהִנֵּה אָנֹכִי עִמָּךְ וּשְׁמַרְתִּיךָ בְּכֹל
אֲשֶׁר־תֵּלֵךְ וַהֲשִׁבֹתִיךָ אֶל־**הָאֲדָמָה הַזֹּאת** כִּי לֹא אֶעֱזָבְךָ עַד
אֲשֶׁר אִם־עָשִׂיתִי אֵת אֲשֶׁר־דִּבַּרְתִּי לָךְ׃ 16 וַיִּיקַץ יַעֲקֹב מִשְּׁנָתוֹ
וַיֹּאמֶר אָכֵן יֵשׁ יְהוָה **בַּמָּקוֹם הַזֶּה** וְאָנֹכִי לֹא יָדָעְתִּי׃ 17 וַיִּירָא
וַיֹּאמַר מַה־נּוֹרָא **הַמָּקוֹם הַזֶּה** אֵין **זֶה** כִּי אִם־בֵּית אֱלֹהִים
וְזֶה שַׁעַר הַשָּׁמָיִם׃

חָרָנָה	—	Haran-ward, toward Haran
בַּמָּקוֹם הַהוּא	—	in that place
אַרְצָה	—	earthward, toward earth
הַשָּׁמַיְמָה	—	heavenward, toward the heavens
יָמָּה	—	seaward, toward the sea
קֵדְמָה	—	eastward, toward the east
צָפֹנָה	—	northward, toward the north
נֶגְבָּה	—	toward the Negev, southward
הָאֲדָמָה הַזֹּאת	—	this land
בַּמָּקוֹם הַזֶּה	—	in this place
הַמָּקוֹם הַזֶּה	—	this place
זֶה	—	this

Additional Reading and Translation Practice

Translate the following excerpts from the Bible and the prayer book, using the extra vocabulary words provided. Check your translations against the English translations that follow.

1. שֶׁהֶחֱיָנוּ—This blessing is said on the first evening of festivals and for other joyous occasions and special events. The word זֶה appears at the end of the blessing.

[he] has kept alive (הִפְעִיל *perfect from the root* ח־י־ה) — הֶחֱיָה

[he] has sustained — קִיֵּם

[he] has caused to reach (הִפְעִיל *perfect form*) — הִגִּיעַ

time/season — זְמַן

בָּרוּךְ אַתָּה יְיָ אֱלֹהֵינוּ מֶלֶךְ הָעוֹלָם, שֶׁהֶחֱיָנוּ וְקִיְּמָנוּ וְהִגִּיעָנוּ
לַזְּמַן הַזֶּה.

2. From the Passover Four Questions—This passage is the opening phrase of the Four Questions recited at the Passover seder. The word זֶה appears with the word לַיְלָה.

what — מַה

differentiates, makes different — נִּשְׁתַּנָּה

מַה נִּשְׁתַּנָּה הַלַּיְלָה הַזֶּה מִכָּל הַלֵּילוֹת?

3. וְזֹאת הַתּוֹרָה—This composite of the biblical verses Deuteronomy 4:44 and Numbers 9:23 is said as the Torah scroll is lifted following the reading of the Torah. Because the word תּוֹרָה is grammatically feminine, the form זֹאת is used.

(he) placed, put — שָׂם

before — לִפְנֵי

according to — עַל פִּי

וְזֹאת הַתּוֹרָה אֲשֶׁר־שָׂם מֹשֶׁה לִפְנֵי בְּנֵי יִשְׂרָאֵל עַל פִּי יְיָ בְּיַד־מֹשֶׁה:

---

4. וְנֶאֱמַר—This passage is the last line of the *Aleinu* prayer. Except for the first word, this is the biblical verse Zechariah 14:9. The word הוּא is used here to mean "that."

and it was said (***from the root*** **א־מ־ר**)	—	וְנֶאֱמַר
will be (***perfect verb with reversing*** **vav** ***from the root*** **ה־י־ה**)	—	וְהָיָה

וְנֶאֱמַר: וְהָיָה יְיָ לְמֶלֶךְ עַל־כָּל־הָאָרֶץ, בַּיּוֹם הַהוּא יִהְיֶה יְיָ אֶחָד וּשְׁמוֹ אֶחָד:

---

5. From Deuteronomy 1:1—This passage begins the fifth book of the Torah.

on the other side of, across	—	בְּעֵבֶר
the Jordan	—	הַיַּרְדֵּן
wilderness	—	מִדְבָּר
in the Aravah	—	בָּעֲרָבָה

אֵלֶּה הַדְּבָרִים אֲשֶׁר דִּבֶּר מֹשֶׁה אֶל־כָּל־יִשְׂרָאֵל בְּעֵבֶר הַיַּרְדֵּן בַּמִּדְבָּר בָּעֲרָבָה....

---

6. מִי כָמֹכָה—This version is included in the evening service. The opening line is the biblical verse Exodus 15:11; the last phrase is Exodus 15:18.

כְּמוֹ, like, ***with a variant form of the ending*** **ךָ, you**	—	כָמֹכָה
with {among} the gods	—	בָּאֵלִם

majestic	—	נֶאְדָּר
awesome (*from the root* י־ר־א)	—	נוֹרָא
splendors	—	תְהִלֹּת
wonder	—	פֶלֶא
sovereignty	—	מַלְכוּת
they saw (*plural form of the root* ר־א־ה)	—	רָאוּ
splitting	—	בּוֹקֵעַ
before	—	לִפְנֵי
my God	—	אֵלִי
they replied	—	עָנוּ

מִי־כָמֹכָה בָּאֵלִם יְיָ, מִי כָּמֹכָה נֶאְדָּר בַּקֹּדֶשׁ, נוֹרָא תְהִלֹּת, עֹשֵׂה פֶלֶא? מַלְכוּתְךָ רָאוּ בָנֶיךָ, בּוֹקֵעַ יָם לִפְנֵי מֹשֶׁה. זֶה אֵלִי עָנוּ וְאָמְרוּ: יְיָ יִמְלֹךְ לְעֹלָם וָעֶד.

____

____

____

____

7. From the Blessing after the Haftarah—This blessing is said following reading of the Haftarah (the weekly or holiday selection from the prophetic books of the Bible). The word זֶה matches the masculine word יוֹם in the word pair יוֹם הַשַּׁבָּת.

about, regarding	—	עַל
service	—	עֲבוֹדָה
you have given (*from the root* נ־ת־ן)	—	נָתַתָּ
give thanks	—	מוֹדִים

עַל־הַתּוֹרָה, וְעַל־הָעֲבוֹדָה, וְעַל־הַנְּבִיאִים, וְעַל־יוֹם הַשַּׁבָּת הַזֶּה, שֶׁנָּתַתָּ־לָּנוּ, יְיָ אֱלֹהֵינוּ...

עַל־הַכֹּל, יְיָ אֱלֹהֵינוּ, אֲנַחְנוּ מוֹדִים לָךְ וּמְבָרְכִים אוֹתָךְ....

____

____

____

____

Translations

1. שֶׁהֶחֱיָנוּ—Blessed are You, Eternal our God, Sovereign of the universe, who has kept us alive and has sustained us and has caused us to reach [to] this time/season.
2. From the Passover Four Questions—What differentiates/makes different this night from all the nights?
3. וְזֹאת הַתּוֹרָה—And this is the Torah that Moses placed before the Children of Israel {Israelites} according to the Eternal in {by} the hand of Moses.
4. וְנֶאֱמַר—And it was said: the Eternal will be Sovereign over all the earth, on that day the Eternal will be one and His {God's} name One.
5. From Deuteronomy 1:1—These are the words that Moses said to all Israel on the other side of the Jordan in the wilderness in the Aravah....
6. מִי כָמֹכָה—Who is like You with {among} the gods, Eternal One, who is like You, majestic in holiness, awesome splendors, doing wonder? Your sovereignty Your children saw {Your children saw Your sovereignty}, splitting [the] sea before Moses. This is my God! they replied and they said: The Eternal shall reign forever and ever!
7. From the Blessing after the Haftarah—Regarding {for} the Torah, and regarding {for} the service, and regarding {for} the prophets and regarding {for} this day of the Sabbath {this Sabbath day}, that You have given to us Eternal our God...regarding {for} the all {everything}, Eternal our God, we give thanks to You and bless You....

Exercises

1. Read and translate the following groups of words.

a. זֶה הַבַּיִת. ______________

זֹאת הַמְּזוּזָה. ______________

אֵלֶּה הַזְּרָעִים. ______________

אֵלֶּה זְרָעֶיךָ. ______________

אֵלֶּה אֲחִיהֶם. ______________

b. זֶה לְבָבוֹ. ______________

זֹאת נַפְשׁוֹ. ______________

אֵלֶּה הַפָּנִים. ______________

אֵלֶּה הַיָּדַיִם. ______________

זֶה רֹאשָׁהּ. ______________

<table>
<tr><td>.d הַמַּלְאָךְ הַזֶּה ______</td><td>.c הַדֶּרֶךְ הַזֹּאת ______</td></tr>
<tr><td>הַמַּלְאָךְ הַהוּא ______</td><td>הַדֶּרֶךְ הַהִיא ______</td></tr>
<tr><td>הַמַּלְאָכִים הָהֵם ______</td><td>הַדְּרָכִים הָאֵלֶּה ______</td></tr>
<tr><td>אֵלֶּה הַמַּלְאָכִים. ______</td><td>הַדְּרָכִים הָהֵן ______</td></tr>
<tr><td>זֶה הַמַּלְאָךְ. ______</td><td>הַדְּבָרִים הָהֵם ______</td></tr>
<tr><td>.f זֶה הָעֵץ. ______</td><td>.e הַיָּם הַגָּדוֹל ______</td></tr>
<tr><td>אֵלֶּה הָעֵצִים. ______</td><td>בַּיָּם הַגָּדוֹל ______</td></tr>
<tr><td>הָעֵץ הַזֶּה ______</td><td>הַיָּם הַזֶּה ______</td></tr>
<tr><td>הָעֵץ הַהוּא ______</td><td>הַיָּם הַהוּא ______</td></tr>
<tr><td>הָעֵצִים הָאֵלֶּה ______</td><td>בַּיָּם הַגָּדוֹל הַזֶּה ______</td></tr>
</table>

2. In each of the following phrases or sentences, circle the one form in the parentheses that is grammatically correct. Translate.

.a הָעַיִן (הָאֵלֶּה, זֶה, הַזֹּאת) ______

.b הַפָּנִים (הַזֶּה, הָאֵלֶּה, זֶה) ______

.c (זֹאת, הָאֵלֶּה, הָהֵם) לֹא הַדֶּרֶךְ. ______

.d (זֶה, הַהוּא, אֵלֶּה) רֵעַךְ. ______

.e אָנֹכִי הָאָדָם (הַזֹּאת, זֶה, הַהוּא). ______

.f אֲנִי מֵהָאֲדָמָה (הַזֹּאת, זֶה, הָהֵם). ______

.g מִי הַחוֹלִים (הָהֵם, הַזֶּה, זֹאת)? ______

.h יֵשׁ צֶדֶק בָּעִיר (זֶה, הַזֹּאת, אֵלֶּה). ______

.i אֵין שָׁלוֹם בָּאָרֶץ (הָאֵלֶּה, הָהֵם, הַהִיא). ______

.j (הַזֹּאת, זֶה, אֵלֶּה) דַּם אָבִינוּ. ______

3. Read and translate the following groups of sentences. Remember the use of the reversing *vav* prefix, introduced in Chapter 2 of *Bet Is for B'reishit*. Check your translations against those that follow.

.a יֵשׁ מַיִם בַּמָּקוֹם הַזֶּה. ______

אֵין רוּחַ בַּמָּקוֹם הַהוּא. ______________________

יֵשׁ נְעָרִים עִם אֲבָנִים שָׁם. ______________________

יֵשׁ הָרִים בֵּין הָעִיר הַזֹּאת וּבֵין הַיָּם. ______________________

____

b. יוֹשְׁבֵי כְּנַעַן יָרְאוּ אֶת הַחֹשֶׁךְ הַהוּא. ______________________

____

זֶה הַחֹשֶׁךְ אֲשֶׁר יָרְאוּ. ______________________

לֹא יָרְאוּ אֶת קוֹל הַנָּבִיא. ______________________

וַיִּירָא הַנָּבִיא אֶת קוֹל הָאֱלֹהִים. ______________________

וַיִּירְאוּ כָּל הַגּוֹיִם אֲשֶׁר שָׁמְעוּ אֶת הַקּוֹל הַהוּא. ______________________

____

c. זֹאת הָאֶבֶן אֲשֶׁר לָקַח הָאָדָם מִן הָהָר. ______________________

____

יִצְחָק לֹא לָקַח אִשָּׁה מֵאֶרֶץ כְּנַעַן. ______________________

____

אֲנִי לוֹקֵחַ אֶת בִּנְךָ עִם מִשְׁפַּחְתּוֹ. ______________________

____

לֹא לָקְחוּ מִיָּדֵינוּ אֶת הָעִיר עַד הַיּוֹם הַזֶּה. ______________________

____

d. וַיֵּלֶךְ יַעֲקֹב בָּעֶרֶב אֶל הַיָּם עִם עֲבָדָיו. ______________________

____

וַתֵּלֶךְ רִבְקָה יָמָּה עִם עֲבָדֶיהָ בְּאוֹר הַיּוֹם. ______________________

____

כָּל שָׁנָה עָלָה הָאִישׁ עַל הָהָר הַזֶּה. ______________________

וְעָלָה הָאִישׁ הָהָרָה וְהֶעֱלָה לֶחֶם וּמַיִם. ____________

e. אֵלֶּה הַדְּבָרִים אֲשֶׁר אָנֹכִי מְצַוֶּה אֶתְכֶם. ____________

אֵלֶּה הַדְּבָרִים שֶׁאֲנִי אוֹמֵר כָּל יוֹם. ____________

הִנְנִי מְהַלֵּל אֶת מַעֲשֵׂה יָדֶיךָ. ____________

וַתְּדַבֵּר הָאֵם וַתְּהַלֵּל אֶת בָּנֶיהָ. ____________

Translations

a. There is water in this place.

There is no wind/spirit in that place.

There are lads/youths/young men with stones there.

There are mountains between this city and [between] the sea.

b. The dwellers {inhabitants} of Canaan feared/did fear/were fearing/had feared/have feared {were in awe of/had been in awe of/have been in awe of} that darkness.

This is the darkness that they feared/did fear/had feared/have feared {were in awe of/had been in awe of/have been in awe of}.

They did not fear/had not feared {were not in awe of/had not been in awe of} the voice of the prophet.

The prophet feared/did fear/was fearing {was in awe of, revered} the voice of God.

All the nations/peoples that heard that voice feared/did fear {were in awe, revered}.

c. This is the stone that the man/human being took from the mountain.

Isaac did not take/was not taking/had not taken a wife from the land of Canaan.

I take/do take/am taking your son with his family.

They did not take from our hands the city until this day.

d. Jacob went/did go/was going {walked/did walk/was walking} in the evening to/toward the sea with his servants/slaves.

Rebekah went/did go/was going {walked/did walk/was walking} seaward {toward the sea} with her servants/slaves in the light of day.

Every year the man went up/was going up/did go up/has gone up/had gone up upon this mountain.

The man will/may go up/ascend mountainward {to the mountain} and he will/may bring up bread and water.

e. These are the words/things that I command/am commanding/do command you.

These are the words that I say/am saying/do say every day.

Here I am/behold me praising the acts/work of your hands.

The mother spoke/did speak/was speaking and she praised/did praise/was praising her children.

FROM OUR TEXTS

Mishnah Pe-ah 1:1

This is the opening passage of tractate Pe-ah of the Mishnah. A variation of this passage appears in the morning service. The first word אֵלּוּ is a postbiblical form of the word אֵלֶּה, "these." The word זֶה, "this," also appears in this passage in the phrase בָּעוֹלָם הַזֶּה, "in this world."

אֵלּוּ דְבָרִים שֶׁאֵין לָהֶם שִׁעוּר:
הַפֵּאָה, וְהַבִּכּוּרִים, וְהָרֵאָיוֹן, וּגְמִילוּת חֲסָדִים, וְתַלְמוּד תּוֹרָה.
אֵלּוּ דְבָרִים שֶׁאָדָם אוֹכֵל פֵּרוֹתֵיהֶן בָּעוֹלָם הַזֶּה וְהַקֶּרֶן קַיֶּמֶת לוֹ לָעוֹלָם הַבָּא:
כִּבּוּד אָב וָאֵם, וּגְמִילוּת חֲסָדִים, וַהֲבָאַת שָׁלוֹם בֵּין אָדָם לַחֲבֵרוֹ וְתַלְמוּד
תּוֹרָה כְּנֶגֶד כֻּלָּם:

These are things that have no limit {deeds for which no limit is specified}:

pe-ah *{leaving the corners of the field for the poor},* bikurim *{offering the first fruits of the season},* rei-ayon *{the pilgrimage offerings in Jerusalem},* g'milut chasadim *{acts of loving-kindness}, and* talmud Torah *{the study of Torah}.*

These are things that a man eats their fruit in this world and the glory endures for him into the next world {These are deeds whose fruitfulness nourishes us in this world and whose merit continues into the world to come}:

honoring father and mother, acts of loving-kindness, bringing peace between a person and his/her fellow {one person and another}, and the study of Torah as opposed to all of them {is equal to all of them}.

Torah Study Text: Exodus 3:1–7

Moses first encounters the Divine Presence in the wilderness at a burning bush. This encounter transforms Moses's destiny from the shepherd of his father-in-law's flocks to the shepherd of the Children of Israel, leading them out of slavery in Egypt.

Read the Hebrew below to see how many of the words you can recognize. This passage does contain words, Hebrew roots, and grammatical concepts that have not yet been introduced. Underline or circle the words, roots, endings, and prefixes that you know.

1 וּמֹשֶׁה הָיָה רֹעֶה אֶת־צֹאן יִתְרוֹ חֹתְנוֹ כֹּהֵן מִדְיָן וַיִּנְהַג אֶת־הַצֹּאן
אַחַר הַמִּדְבָּר וַיָּבֹא אֶל־הַר הָאֱלֹהִים חֹרֵבָה׃ 2 וַיֵּרָא מַלְאַךְ יְהוָה
אֵלָיו בְּלַבַּת־אֵשׁ מִתּוֹךְ הַסְּנֶה וַיַּרְא וְהִנֵּה הַסְּנֶה בֹּעֵר בָּאֵשׁ
וְהַסְּנֶה אֵינֶנּוּ אֻכָּל׃ 3 וַיֹּאמֶר מֹשֶׁה אָסֻרָה־נָּא וְאֶרְאֶה אֶת־הַמַּרְאֶה
הַגָּדֹל הַזֶּה מַדּוּעַ לֹא־יִבְעַר הַסְּנֶה׃ 4 וַיַּרְא יְהוָה כִּי סָר לִרְאוֹת
וַיִּקְרָא אֵלָיו אֱלֹהִים מִתּוֹךְ הַסְּנֶה וַיֹּאמֶר מֹשֶׁה מֹשֶׁה וַיֹּאמֶר
הִנֵּנִי׃ 5 וַיֹּאמֶר אַל־תִּקְרַב הֲלֹם שַׁל־נְעָלֶיךָ מֵעַל רַגְלֶיךָ כִּי הַמָּקוֹם
אֲשֶׁר אַתָּה עוֹמֵד עָלָיו אַדְמַת־קֹדֶשׁ הוּא׃ 6 וַיֹּאמֶר אָנֹכִי אֱלֹהֵי
אָבִיךָ אֱלֹהֵי אַבְרָהָם אֱלֹהֵי יִצְחָק וֵאלֹהֵי יַעֲקֹב וַיַּסְתֵּר מֹשֶׁה פָּנָיו
כִּי יָרֵא מֵהַבִּיט אֶל־הָאֱלֹהִים׃ 7 וַיֹּאמֶר יְהוָה רָאֹה רָאִיתִי אֶת־עֳנִי
עַמִּי אֲשֶׁר בְּמִצְרָיִם וְאֶת־צַעֲקָתָם שָׁמַעְתִּי מִפְּנֵי נֹגְשָׂיו כִּי יָדַעְתִּי
אֶת־מַכְאֹבָיו׃

Translating the Torah Study Text

Following is our Torah Study Text, Exodus 3:1–7, reprinted with a literal translation underneath each word. Using your knowledge of the building blocks of the Hebrew language and the meanings of the words provided below, translate this passage into clear English sentences. Write your translation on the lines following the text. This selection includes some grammatical forms and vocabulary that have not yet been introduced. You will need to rely, in part, on the translations provided.

Exodus 3:1–7

וּמֹשֶׁה	הָיָה	רֹעֶה	אֶת־צֹאן	יִתְרוֹ	חֹתְנוֹ	כֹּהֵן	מִדְיָן
and Moses	*was*	*shepherding*	*flock*	*Jethro*	*his father-in-law*	*priest*	*Midian*

וַיִּנְהַג	אֶת־הַצֹּאן	אַחַר	הַמִּדְבָּר	וַיָּבֹא	אֶל־	הַר
and he drove/ guided/led	*the flock*	*behind*	*the wilderness*	*and he came*	*to*	*mountain*

הָאֱלֹהִים	חֹרֵבָה׃	וַיֵּרָא	מַלְאַךְ	יְהוָה	אֵלָיו	בְּלַבַּת־
(the) God	*to/toward Horeb*	*appeared*	*angel/ messenger*	*the Eternal*	*to him*	*in flame*

אֵשׁ	מִתּוֹךְ	הַסְּנֶה	וַיַּרְא	וְהִנֵּה	הַסְּנֶה	בֹּעֵר
fire	*out of/from the midst of*	*the bush*	*and he saw*	*and behold/ here is*	*the bush*	*burning*

בָּאֵשׁ	וְהַסְּנֶה	אֵינֶנּוּ	אֻכָּל׃	וַיֹּאמֶר	מֹשֶׁה	אָסֻרָה־
in the fire	*and the bush*	*not*	*consumed*	*and said*	*Moses*	*let me/I will turn aside*

נָּא	וְאֶרְאֶה	אֶת־הַמַּרְאֶה	הַגָּדֹל	הַזֶּה	מַדּוּעַ	לֹא־	יִבְעַר	הַסְּנֶה׃
now	*and see*	*sight*	*great*	*this*	*why*	*not*	*burn*	*the bush*

וַיַּרְא	יְהוָה	כִּי	סָר	לִרְאוֹת	וַיִּקְרָא	אֵלָיו	אֱלֹהִים
and saw	*the Eternal*	*that*	*he turned aside*	*to see*	*and called*	*to him*	*God*

מִתּוֹךְ	הַסְּנֶה	וַיֹּאמֶר	מֹשֶׁה	מֹשֶׁה	וַיֹּאמֶר	הִנֵּנִי׃
out of/from the midst of	*the bush*	*and he said*	*Moses*	*Moses*	*and he said*	*here I am*

וַיֹּאמֶר	אַל־	תִּקְרַב	הֲלֹם	שַׁל־	נְעָלֶיךָ	מֵעַל	רַגְלֶיךָ
and he said	*do not*	*come near*	*to here*	*remove*	*your shoes*	*from upon*	*your feet*

כִּי	הַמָּקוֹם	אֲשֶׁר	אַתָּה	עוֹמֵד	עָלָיו	אַדְמַת־	קֹדֶשׁ	הוּא׃	וַיֹּאמֶר
for	*the place*	*that*	*you*	*stand*	*upon it*	*ground of*	*holiness*	*it*	*and he said*

אָנֹכִי	אֱלֹהֵי	אָבִיךָ	אֱלֹהֵי	אַבְרָהָם	אֱלֹהֵי	יִצְחָק	וֵאלֹהֵי	יַעֲקֹב
I	*God of*	*your father*	*God of*	*Abraham*	*God of*	*Isaac*	*and God of*	*Jacob*

וַיַּסְתֵּר	מֹשֶׁה	פָּנָיו	כִּי	יָרֵא	מֵהַבִּיט	אֶל־	הָאֱלֹהִים׃
and hid	*Moses*	*his face*	*for*	*he was afraid/ in awe*	*of looking*	*at*	*God*

וַיֹּאמֶר	יְהוָה	רָאֹה	רָאִיתִי	אֶת־עֳנִי	עַמִּי	אֲשֶׁר
and said	*the Eternal*	*see* (emphasis)	*I have seen*	*the affliction*	*my people*	*who/that*

כִּי	נֹגְשָׂיו	מִפְּנֵי	שָׁמַעְתִּי	וְאֶת־צַעֲקָתָם	בְּמִצְרָיִם
for	*its taskmasters*	*because of*	*I have heard*	*their cry and*	*in Egypt*

אֶת־מַכְאֹבָיו׃	יָדַעְתִּי
its sufferings	*I have known*

TORAH Translations

Compare your translation of Exodus 3:1–7 with the Torah translations below.

[1]Now Moses, tending the flock of his father-in-law Jethro, the priest of Midian, drove the flock into the wilderness, and came to Horeb, the mountain of God. [2]An angel of the LORD appeared to him in a blazing fire out of a bush. He gazed, and there was a bush all aflame, yet the bush was not consumed. [3]Moses said, "I must turn aside to look at this marvelous sight; why doesn't the bush burn up?" [4]When the LORD saw that he had turned aside to look, God called to him out of the bush: "Moses! Moses!" He answered, "Here I am." [5]And He said, "Do not come closer. Remove your sandals from your feet, for the place on which you stand is holy ground. [6]I am," He said, "the God of your father, the God of Abraham, the God of Isaac, and the God of Jacob." And Moses hid his face, for he was afraid to look at God.

[7]And the LORD continued, "I have marked well the plight of My people in Egypt and have heeded their outcry because of their taskmasters; yes, I am mindful of their sufferings.

JPS Hebrew-English Tanakh: The Traditional Hebrew Text and the New JPS Translation—2d Ed. Philadelphia: Jewish Publication Society, 1999.

Moses was shepherding the sheep of Jethro, his father-in-law, the priest of Midian; he guided the sheep far into the wilderness, and he arrived at the Mountain of God, toward Horeb. [2]An angel of God appeared to him in a blaze of fire from amid the bush. He saw and behold! the bush was burning in the fire but the bush was not consumed. [3]Moses thought, "I will turn aside now and look at this great sight—why will the bush not be burned?"

[4]HASHEM saw that he turned aside to see; and God called out to him from amid the bush and said, "Moses, Moses," and he replied, "Here I am!" [5]He said, "Do not come closer to here, remove your shoes from your feet, for the place upon which you stand is

holy ground." [6]*And He said, "I am the God of your father, the God of Abraham, the God of Isaac, and the God of Jacob." Moses hid his face, for he was afraid to gaze toward God.*

[7]*HASHEM said, "I have indeed seen the affliction of My people that is in Egypt and I have heard its outcry because of its taskmasters, for I have known of its sufferings.*

THE *CHUMASH*, ARTSCROLL SERIES, STONE EDITION. BROOKLYN: MESORAH PUBLICATIONS, 1993.

[1]*Now Moshe was shepherding the flock of Yitro his father-in-law, priest of Midyan.*
He led the flock behind the wilderness—
and he came to the mountain of God, to Horev.
[2]*And YHWH's messenger was seen by him*
in the flame of a fire out of the midst of a bush.
He saw:
here, the bush is burning with fire,
and the bush is not consumed!
[3]*Moshe said:*
Now let me turn aside
that I may see this great sight—
why the bush does not burn up!
[4]*When YHWH saw that he had turned aside to see,*
God called to him out of the midst of the bush,
he said:
Moshe! Moshe!
He said:
Here I am.
[5]*He said:*
Do not come near to here,
put off your sandal from your foot,
for the place on which you stand—it is holy ground!
[6]*And he said:*
I am the God of your father,
the God of Avraham,
the God of Yitzhak,
and the God of Yaakov.
Moshe concealed his face,
for he was afraid to gaze upon God.
[7]*Now YHWH said:*

I have seen, yes, seen the affliction of my people that is in Egypt,
their cry have I heard in the face of their slave-drivers;
indeed, I have known their sufferings!

The Five Books of Moses: A New Translation with Introductions, Commentary and Notes by Everett Fox. New York: Schocken Books, 1995.

Now Moshe kept the flock of Yitro his father in law, the priest of Midyan: and he led the flock far away into the desert, and came to the mountain of God, to Horev. And the angel of the Lord appeared to him in a flame of fire out of the midst of a bush: and he looked, and, behold, the bush burned with fire, but the bush was not consumed. And Moshe said, I will now turn aside, and see this great sight, why the bush is not burnt. And when the Lord saw that he turned aside to see, God called to him out of the midst of the bush, and said, Moshe, Moshe. And he said, Here I am. And he said, Do not come near: put off thy shoes from off thy feet, for the place on which thou dost stand is holy ground. Moreover, he said, I am the God of thy father, the God of Avraham, the God of Yizhaq, and the God of Ya'aqov. And Moshe hid his face; for he was afraid to look upon God. And the Lord said, I have surely seen the affliction of my people who are in Mizrayim, and have heard their cry by reason of their taskmasters; for I know their sorrows....

The Jerusalem Bible, published for the Nahum Zeev Williams Family Foundation at Hechal Shlomo, Jerusalem. Jerusalem: Koren Publishers Jerusalem Ltd., 1969.

Vocabulary

Locate each of the following words in the Torah Study Text: Exodus 3:1–7.

priest *m*	—	כֹּהֵן
after, behind	—	אַחַר
wilderness, desert *m*	—	מִדְבָּר
fire *f*	—	אֵשׁ
midst of, middle of	—	תּוֹךְ
because, for; that	—	כִּי

Note on the Vocabulary

The word תּוֹךְ is actually the word-pair form of תָּוֶךְ, a word meaning "midst"or "middle." It appears most often as בְּתוֹךְ, "in the midst of" or "within," or as מִתּוֹךְ, "from the midst of," "out of," or "from among."

The root ר־א־ה most often appears in the פָּעַל pattern, where it has the basic meaning "see." It does appear in other verb patterns, where it has related meanings, such as "appear" or "seem." In the הִפְעִיל pattern, for example, it means "cause to see" or "show." The participle, perfect, and imperfect forms of the root ר־א־ה in both the פָּעַל and הִפְעִיל patterns can be found in the verb charts in the back of the book.

The root ר־א־ה appears several times in this chapter's Torah Study Text. The final root letter ה drops out in many words formed from this root.

(verse 2)

a messenger/angel of the Eternal appeared to him — וַיֵּרָא מַלְאַךְ יְהוָה אֵלָיו

(verse 2)

and he saw and behold/here the bush burning — וַיַּרְא וְהִנֵּה הַסְּנֶה בֹּעֵר

(verse 3)

and I will see this great sight — וְאֶרְאֶה אֶת־הַמַּרְאֶה הַגָּדֹל הַזֶּה

(verse 4)

and the Eternal saw that he had turned aside to see — וַיַּרְא יְהוָה כִּי סָר לִרְאוֹת

(verse 7)

see (*emphasis*) I have seen the affliction of my people — רָאֹה רָאִיתִי אֶת־עֳנִי עַמִּי

Words from the root ר־א־ה can be easily confused with words from the root י־ר־א, "fear/revere/be in awe," introduced in the last chapter. The context, however, can help determine which root it is. It is the root י־ר־א that appears in verse 6:

And Moses hid his face for he was afraid/in awe of looking at God. — וַיַּסְתֵּר מֹשֶׁה פָּנָיו כִּי יָרֵא מֵהַבִּיט אֶל־הָאֱלֹהִים׃

The following words, both ancient and modern, are derived from the root ר־א־ה. The final root letter ה drops out in many words formed from this root.

seer; prophetic vision	—	רֹאֶה
mirror	—	רְאִי
sight, appearance, vision	—	מַרְאֶה
Reuben (*literally:* see, a son!)	—	רְאוּבֵן
see you again! so long! (*literally:* to see each other)	—	לְהִתְרָאוֹת
exhibition, show	—	רַאֲוָה
seemly, suitable, appropriate	—	רָאוּי
seeing, sight, view; visibility	—	רְאוּת
sight, vision	—	רְאִיָּה
proof, evidence	—	רְאָיָה
semblance, impression, appearance	—	מַרְאִית עַיִן

THE ROOT ב־ו־א

The basic meaning of the root ב־ו־א is "come." This root follows the פָּעַל pattern, with some variations caused by the middle root letter ו. It also appears in the הִפְעִיל pattern with the meaning "cause to come" or "bring." The participle, perfect, and imperfect forms of the root ב־ו־א in both the פָּעַל and הִפְעִיל patterns can be found in the verb charts in the back of the book.

The root ב־ו־א appears once in our Torah Study Text. The root letter ו has dropped out:

(verse 1)

and he came to the mountain of God — וַיָּבֹא אֶל־הַר הָאֱלֹהִים

The following words and expressions, both ancient and modern, are derived from the root ב־ו־א. The middle root letter ו drops out or appears as the vowel וֹ or וּ in many words formed from this root.

entrance; input; preface	—	מָבוֹא
product, yield	—	תְּבוּאָה
the world to come, the hereafter {the coming world, eternity}	—	הָעוֹלָם הַבָּא

next year, the coming year	—	הַשָּׁנָה הַבָּאָה
welcome! {blessed are the ones who come}	—	בְּרוּכִים הַבָּאִים
peacemaking {bringing of peace, causing peace to come}	—	הֲבָאַת שָׁלוֹם

TORAH Commentary

Verse 2 states וַיַּרְא*, "and he saw," but there is no object for the verb* וַיַּרְא*. The verse immediately states,* וְהִנֵּה הַסְּנֶה בֹּעֵר בָּאֵשׁ וְהַסְּנֶה אֵינֶנּוּ אֻכָּל*, "and behold the bush was burning in the fire and the bush was not consumed." What was it that Moses actually saw?*

The story is customarily offered as a "miracle" that God performed to get Moses' attention. This fails to explain why God, who could split the sea, fashion pillars of fire, and make the sun stand still, would resort to something so trivial and undramatic to attract Moses' attention as to make a bush burn without being consumed. It is a cheap trick.

Look more closely at the process of combustion. How long would you have to watch wood burn before you could know whether or not it actually was being consumed? Even dry kindling wood is not burned up for several minutes. This then would mean that Moses would have had to watch the "amazing sight" closely for several minutes before he could possibly know there was even a miracle to watch! (The producers of television commercials, who have a lot invested in knowing the span of human visual attention, seem to agree that one minute is our outer limit.)

The "burning bush" was not a miracle. It was a test. God wanted to find out whether or not Moses could pay attention to something for more than a few minutes. When Moses did, God spoke. The trick is to pay attention to what is going on around you long enough to behold the miracle without falling asleep. There is another world, right here within this one, whenever we pay attention.

LAWRENCE KUSHNER, *GOD WAS IN THIS PLACE & I, I DID NOT KNOW.* WOODSTOCK, VT.: JEWISH LIGHTS PUBLISHING, 1993.

In verse 3, Moses says, אָסֻרָה־נָּא וְאֶרְאֶה, "Let me/I will turn aside now and see." The words אָסֻרָה־נָּא, "Let me/I will turn aside now," are somewhat superfluous, as the text could have simply stated אֶרְאֶה, "Let me/I will see." The inclusion of the words אָסֻרָה־נָּא has, therefore, been viewed midrashically as an indication of Moses' willingness to turn from his own path to serve God. The following commentary expands upon this midrashic idea.

The Midrash *lauds Moshe's actions, as he "exerted" himself to see the wondrous sight. R. Yochanon says that Moshe took three steps out of his way, while Reish Lakish says that he turned his head to gaze at the remarkable burning bush. We can glean a deeper understanding of Moshe's action as stated by the* Midrash....

Man is not expected to complete the entire endeavor. All that is demanded of him is that initial effort, the desire to perform for Hashem. The rest will be realized through Hashem's assistance. In the Midrash Shir Ha'Shirim, Chazal *state:* "Hashem says, 'Open for Me an opening the size of the eye of a needle and I will open for you entrances through which wagons may enter.'" *The Almighty waits for us to initiate the relationship, to take that first step. As soon as we demonstrate our willingness to grow spiritually, as soon as we concretize our aspirations in any small measure, we have endeavored to move nearer to Hashem. We have thereby created a tiny entrance. Hashem will complete the task.*

RABBI A. L. SCHEINBAUM, *PENINIM ON THE TORAH*. CLEVELAND: PENINIM PUBLICATIONS, 2000.

In verse 5, Moses is told, הַמָּקוֹם אֲשֶׁר אַתָּה עוֹמֵד עָלָיו, "the place that you are standing upon it" is holy ground. Why does it specify אֲשֶׁר אַתָּה עוֹמֵד?

Why does it say that "the place on which you *stand is holy ground"? Surely one would assume that the holy ground is the soil underneath the burning bush, not the sand underneath Moses' feet several yards away from the bush. "The place on which* you *stand is holy" teaches us that holiness is found not in the burning bush, not in the extraordinary event, but in the place where* we *stand. Holiness is found in the place, every place and any place, where there stands a human being who is open to an encounter with the Source of Holiness, who is able to apprehend the Divine in the surrounding world.*

BEGINNING THE JOURNEY: A WOMEN'S COMMENTARY ON THE TORAH, ED. RABBI EMILY H. FEIGENSON. NEW YORK: WOMEN OF REFORM JUDAISM, FEDERATION OF TEMPLE SISTERHOODS, 1997.

Exercises

1. Make flash cards for each of the new vocabulary words and Hebrew roots introduced in this chapter, or use the flash card set published as a companion to this book. Review the cards to learn all of them.

2. Draw a line connecting each Hebrew word to its English translation. For some words, there can be more than one correct translation.

midst of	מִדְבָּר
after	
that	כִּי
because	
wilderness	אַחַר
fire	תּוֹךְ
behind	
priest	כֹּהֵן
desert	
for	אֵשׁ

3. On the left are plural forms of words introduced as vocabulary in this chapter. Draw a line connecting each plural word to its singular form. Translate both into English.

________________	מִדְבָּרוֹת	מִדְבָּר	________________
________________	אִשִּׁים		
		כֹּהֵן	________________
________________	מִדְבָּרִים		
________________	כֹּהֲנִים	אֵשׁ	________________

4. Read and translate the following groups of words.

a. הַכֹּהֵן הַגָּדוֹל ________________
כֹּהֵן וְנָבִיא ________________
בְּיַד הַכֹּהֵן ________________
עֵינֵי הַכֹּהֵן ________________
כֹּהֲנֵיהֶם ________________

b. בַּמִּדְבָּר ________________
דֶּרֶךְ הַמִּדְבָּר ________________
מִדְבַּר הָרִים ________________
מִדְבַּר מִצְרָיִם ________________
מִדְבַּר הָעַמִּים ________________

c. אַחַר זֶה ______________
אַחַר הַדָּבָר הַזֶּה ______________
אַחַר הַשַּׁבָּת ______________
אַחַר הָרוּחַ ______________
אַחַר אֶחָיו ______________

d. דָּם וָאֵשׁ ______________
בָּאֵשׁ וּבַמַּיִם ______________
אֵשׁ אֱלֹהִים ______________
אוֹר אֵשׁ ______________
אַבְנֵי אֵשׁ ______________

e. בְּתוֹכוֹ ______________
מִתּוֹכָהּ ______________
בְּתוֹכֵנוּ ______________
מִתּוֹכְכֶם ______________
בְּתוֹכָם ______________

5. Identify the root of each of the following verbs and whether it is a perfect, imperfect, or participle form. Translate.

Verb	Root	Form	Translation
שָׁמְעוּ	______	______	______
הָיוּ	______	______	______
עָלוּ	______	______	______
לָקַח	______	______	______
רָאָה	______	______	______
רָאוּ	______	______	______
רוֹאִים	______	______	______
בָּאוּ	______	______	______
יָבוֹא	______	______	______
תָּבוֹא	______	______	______
תְּהַלֵּל	______	______	______
יֹאמְרוּ	______	______	______

EXTRA CREDIT
Layers of Meaning in Torah Study

The Torah can be studied on many different levels. Four different types of Torah study, four different levels of interpretation, have traditionally been identified by the words פְּשָׁט, רֶמֶז, דְּרָשׁ, and סוֹד.

The word פְּשָׁט, "simple," refers to the plain or literal meaning of the text. Every passage can be understood simply according to its פְּשָׁט, the plain sense of the words and grammar structures themselves.

The word רֶמֶז, "hint" or "allusion," refers to allegorical interpretations of the meaning of a passage.

The word דְּרָשׁ, "homily" or "exposition," refers to midrashic elaborations upon the details of a text, while the word סוֹד, "secret," refers to its hidden, mystical meanings.

The first letters of each of these four words spell the word פַּרְדֵּס, derived from the same root as "paradise" and meaning "garden" or "fruit orchard." "Entering the *pardes*" became the euphemism for engaging in mystical study of the hidden meanings of the Torah, an endeavor that was regarded as fraught with danger. In the Talmud, tractate *Chagigah* 14b, a story is related of four Sages who entered the *pardes:* Ben Azzai, Ben Zoma, Acher (Elisha ben Avuyah), and Akiva. Ben Azzai died, Ben Zoma went crazy, and Elisha ben Avuyah lost his faith and became an apostate (and was henceforth known, not by his name, but as Acher, "Other"). Only the great Sage Akiva was able to enter and depart from the *pardes* in peace.

Torah Study Text: Vocabulary and Root Review

This unit's Torah Study Text, Exodus 3:1–7, is reprinted below, highlighting the new vocabulary words as well as the words formed from the new Hebrew roots introduced in Chapter 3. Read this passage again, recalling the meaning of each of the highlighted words or roots.

1 וּמֹשֶׁה הָיָה רֹעֶה אֶת־צֹאן יִתְרוֹ חֹתְנוֹ **כֹּהֵן** מִדְיָן וַיִּנְהַג אֶת־הַצֹּאן
אַחַר הַמִּדְבָּר וַיָּבֹא אֶל־הַר הָאֱלֹהִים חֹרֵבָה׃ 2 **וַיֵּרָא** מַלְאַךְ יְהוָה
אֵלָיו בְּלַבַּת־**אֵשׁ מִתּוֹךְ** הַסְּנֶה **וַיַּרְא** וְהִנֵּה הַסְּנֶה בֹּעֵר **בָּאֵשׁ**
וְהַסְּנֶה אֵינֶנּוּ אֻכָּל׃ 3 וַיֹּאמֶר מֹשֶׁה אָסֻרָה־נָּא **וְאֶרְאֶה** אֶת־**הַמַּרְאֶה**
הַגָּדֹל הַזֶּה מַדּוּעַ לֹא־יִבְעַר הַסְּנֶה׃ 4 **וַיַּרְא** יְהוָה **כִּי** סָר **לִרְאוֹת**
וַיִּקְרָא אֵלָיו אֱלֹהִים **מִתּוֹךְ** הַסְּנֶה וַיֹּאמֶר מֹשֶׁה מֹשֶׁה וַיֹּאמֶר
הִנֵּנִי׃ 5 וַיֹּאמֶר אַל־תִּקְרַב הֲלֹם שַׁל־נְעָלֶיךָ מֵעַל רַגְלֶיךָ **כִּי** הַמָּקוֹם
אֲשֶׁר אַתָּה עוֹמֵד עָלָיו אַדְמַת־קֹדֶשׁ הוּא׃ 6 וַיֹּאמֶר אָנֹכִי אֱלֹהֵי
אָבִיךָ אֱלֹהֵי אַבְרָהָם אֱלֹהֵי יִצְחָק וֵאלֹהֵי יַעֲקֹב וַיַּסְתֵּר מֹשֶׁה פָּנָיו
כִּי יָרֵא מֵהַבִּיט אֶל־הָאֱלֹהִים׃ 7 וַיֹּאמֶר יְהוָה **רָאֹה רָאִיתִי** אֶת־עֳנִי
עַמִּי אֲשֶׁר בְּמִצְרָיִם וְאֶת־צַעֲקָתָם שָׁמַעְתִּי מִפְּנֵי נֹגְשָׂיו **כִּי** יָדַעְתִּי
אֶת־מַכְאֹבָיו׃

Building Blocks

אֲנִי and אָנֹכִי Verb Forms

In the last unit, we introduced the pronouns אֲנִי and אָנֹכִי, both of which mean "I" and can be used for either masculine or feminine subjects. In Hebrew, there are distinct אֲנִי or אָנֹכִי perfect and imperfect verb forms.

Perfect Forms: The תִּי Ending

The ending תִּי (or, in some cases, תִי) attached to a verb indicates that the verb is a perfect אֲנִי or אָנֹכִי form. This same ending is used with all the Hebrew verb patterns. Following are examples of פָּעַל, פִּעֵל, and הִפְעִיל verbs with this ending attached:

I worked/served	—	עָבַדְתִּי
I spoke	—	דִּבַּרְתִּי
I trusted/believed	—	הֶאֱמַנְתִּי

Remember that perfect verbs describe action that has been completed and can be translated in several different ways. For example, דִּבַּרְתִּי could be translated as "I did speak," "I was speaking," "I had spoken," or "I have spoken."

Imperfect Forms: The א Prefix

The prefix א attached to a verb indicates that the verb is an imperfect אֲנִי or אָנֹכִי form. This same prefix is used with all the Hebrew verb patterns. The vowels appearing under the prefix א vary, depending on the verb pattern and root letters. Following are examples of פָּעַל, פִּעֵל, and הִפְעִיל verbs with this prefix attached:

I will/may work/serve	—	אֶעֱבֹד
I will/may speak	—	אֲדַבֵּר
I will/may trust/believe	—	אַאֲמִין

Remember that imperfect verbs can indicate the future tense, ongoing incompleted action, or action that is wished or urged. So, for example, אֲדַבֵּר could be translated as "I will speak," "I may speak," "may I speak," or "let me speak."

The Endings ִי and ַי and נִי

In *Aleph Isn't Enough* and in *Bet is for B'reishit*, we introduced several pronoun endings, such as ךָ, meaning "your" or "you," and ֶם and הֶם, meaning "their" or "them." In this chapter, we introduce the endings ִי and ַי and נִי. When attached to a preposition, these endings mean "me." Examples:

Prepositions

with me	—	עִמִּי	⟵	with	— עִם
between me, among me	—	בֵּינִי	⟵	between, among	— בֵּין
to me, toward me	—	אֵלַי	⟵	to, toward	— אֶל
like me, as me	—	כָּמוֹנִי	⟵	like, as	— כְּמוֹ

Verbs

The ending נִי also means "me" when attached to a verb. The following example is from the Sabbath hymn, *Shalom Aleichem*.

bless	—	בָּרְכוּ
bless me	—	בָּרְכוּנִי

בָּרְכוּנִי לְשָׁלוֹם, מַלְאֲכֵי הַשָּׁלוֹם, מַלְאֲכֵי עֶלְיוֹן....

Bless me for peace, angels/messengers of peace, angels/messengers of [the] Supreme One....

Nouns

The ִי and ַי endings are attached to nouns. When attached to a noun, these endings mean "my." The ִי ending is used with singular nouns, and the ַי ending is used with plural nouns. Examples:

my brother	—	אָחִי	⟵	brother	— אָח
my brothers	—	אַחַי	⟵	brothers	— אַחִים
my commandments	—	מִצְוֹתַי	⟵	commandments	— מִצְוֹת

Torah Study Text with Building Blocks

Following are excerpts, Exodus 3:3–4 and 7, from this unit's Torah Study Text, reprinted with the new Building Blocks highlighted. Reread these verses, noting the appearance of אֲנִי or אָנֹכִי perfect and imperfect verb forms, and the use of the ִי and נִי endings. A translation is provided below for only the highlighted Building Blocks. Remember that there could be other possible translations. For a full translation of the verses, refer back to Chapter 3.

Exodus 3:3–4

3 וַיֹּאמֶר מֹשֶׁה **אָסֻרָה**־נָּא **וְאֶרְאֶה** אֶת־הַמַּרְאֶה הַגָּדֹל הַזֶּה מַדּוּעַ
לֹא־יִבְעַר הַסְּנֶה׃ 4 וַיַּרְא יְהוָה כִּי סָר לִרְאוֹת וַיִּקְרָא אֵלָיו אֱלֹהִים
מִתּוֹךְ הַסְּנֶה וַיֹּאמֶר מֹשֶׁה מֹשֶׁה וַיֹּאמֶר **הִנֵּנִי**׃

Exodus 3:7

7 וַיֹּאמֶר יְהוָה רָאֹה **רָאִיתִי** אֶת־עֳנִי **עַמִּי** אֲשֶׁר בְּמִצְרָיִם
וְאֶת־צַעֲקָתָם **שָׁמַעְתִּי** מִפְּנֵי נֹגְשָׂיו כִּי **יָדַעְתִּי** אֶת־מַכְאֹבָיו׃

let me/I will turn aside	—	אָסֻרָה
I will/may see	—	אֶרְאֶה
here I am (הִנֵּה ***with*** נִי ***ending attached*)**	—	הִנֵּנִי
I have seen	—	רָאִיתִי
my people	—	עַמִּי
I have heard	—	שָׁמַעְתִּי
I have known	—	יָדַעְתִּי

GRAMMAR Enrichment

Perfect and Imperfect Forms

The following charts include the אֲנִי or אָנֹכִי ("I") forms in the perfect and imperfect for all the roots introduced thus far in this book and in *Bet Is for B'reishit*. פָּעַל, פִּעֵל, and הִפְעִיל verb patterns are included. These are presented for enrichment only. It is not necessary to memorize the information on these charts.

It may be helpful to notice certain variations:

- In roots that end with the letter ה, such as ב־נ־ה, ה־י־ה, ר־א־ה, ע־ל־ה, ח־י־ה, and צ־ו־ה, the root letter ה drops out in all the perfect אֲנִי forms. This also happens with the letter ו when it is the middle root letter, as in the root ב־ו־א.
- In many roots that begin with the letters י, נ, or א, such as א־מ־ר, י־ד־ע, י־צ־א, י־ש־ב, and נ־ת־ן, that first root letter drops out in the imperfect forms.

פָּעַל Verbs

Imperfect	Perfect	Root	Meaning
אֹמַר	אָמַרְתִּי	א־מ־ר	say
אָבוֹא	בָּאתִי	ב־ו־א	come
אֶבְנֶה	בָּנִיתִי	ב־נ־ה	build
אֶהְיֶה	הָיִיתִי	ה־י־ה	be
אֵלֵךְ	הָלַכְתִּי	ה־ל־ך	walk, go
אֵדַע	יָדַעְתִּי	י־ד־ע	know
אִירָא	יָרֵאתִי	י־ר־א	fear, revere, be in awe
אֵשֵׁב	יָשַׁבְתִּי	י־ש־ב	sit, dwell
אֶקַּח	לָקַחְתִּי	ל־ק־ח	take
אֶעֱבֹד	עָבַדְתִּי	ע־ב־ד	work, serve
אֶעֱלֶה	עָלִיתִי	ע־ל־ה	go up, ascend
אֶרְאֶה	רָאִיתִי	ר־א־ה	see

פִּעֵל Verbs

Imperfect	Perfect	Root	Meaning
אֲבָרֵךְ	בֵּרַכְתִּי	ב־ר־ך	bless
אֲדַבֵּר	דִּבַּרְתִּי	ד־ב־ר	speak, talk

אֲהַלֵּל	הִלַּלְתִּי	ה־ל־ל	praise
אֲחַיֶּה	חִיִּיתִי	ח־י־ה	bring to life
אֲצַוֶּה	צִוִּיתִי	צ־ו־ה	command, order
אֲקַדֵּשׁ	קִדַּשְׁתִּי	ק־ד־שׁ	make holy

הִפְעִיל Verbs

Imperfect	Perfect	Root	Meaning
אָבִיא	הֵבֵאתִי	ב־ו־א	cause to come, bring
אוֹלִיךְ	הוֹלַכְתִּי	ה־ל־ך	cause to go, lead, conduct
אַחֲיֶה	הֶחֱיֵיתִי	ח־י־ה	keep alive
אוֹדִיעַ	הוֹדַעְתִּי	י־ד־ע	make known, announce
אוֹצִיא	הוֹצֵאתִי	י־צ־א	cause to go out, bring out
אוֹשִׁיב	הוֹשַׁבְתִּי	י־שׁ־ב	cause to sit *or* dwell, seat
אַעֲבִיד	הֶעֱבַדְתִּי	ע־ב־ד	put to work, employ
אַעֲלֶה	הֶעֱלֵיתִי	ע־ל־ה	cause to ascend, bring up
אַרְאֶה	הֶרְאֵיתִי	ר־א־ה	cause to see, show

Additional Reading and Translation Practice

Translate the following excerpts from the Bible and the prayer book, using the extra vocabulary words provided. Check your translations against the English translations that follow.

1. Psalm 23:1—This is the first verse of one of the most well-known psalms. The ִי ending, meaning "my," and the imperfect א prefix appear in this verse.

a song of/for	—	מִזְמוֹר לְ
David	—	דָּוִד
shepherd	—	רֹעֶה
אֲנִי ***imperfect form from the root*** **ח־ס־ר (lack, be wanting)**	—	אֶחְסָר

מִזְמוֹר לְדָוִד

יְהוָה רֹעִי לֹא אֶחְסָר:

---

2. כִּי אֶשְׁמְרָה שַׁבָּת—In this Shabbat song, the ending נִי, meaning "me," appears twice. The root שׁ־מ־ר appears in both אֲנִי and הוּא imperfect forms.

sign	—	אוֹת
it, she	—	הִיא
לְעוֹלָם וָעֶד	=	לְעוֹלְמֵי עַד

כִּי אֶשְׁמְרָה שַׁבָּת אֵל יִשְׁמְרֵנִי. אוֹת הִיא לְעוֹלְמֵי עַד בֵּינוֹ וּבֵינִי:

---

3. From Psalm 121:1–2—These verses have been set to music and are sung in some liturgical settings. The ִי and ַי endings, meaning "my," and the imperfect א prefix appear in these verses.

אֲנִי *imperfect form from the root* נ־שׂ־א, lift up, raise	—	אֶשָּׂא
from where	—	מֵאַיִן
הוּא *imperfect form from the root* ב־ו־א, come	—	יָבֹא
help, assistance	—	עֵזֶר
from	—	מֵעִם

...אֶשָּׂא עֵינַי אֶל־הֶהָרִים מֵאַיִן יָבֹא עֶזְרִי:
עֶזְרִי מֵעִם יְהוָה עֹשֵׂה שָׁמַיִם וָאָרֶץ:

---

4. From Havdalah (Isaiah 12:2)—This passage is the first of a series of biblical verses included in the introduction to *Havdalah*, the ritual marking the end of Shabbat.

salvation	—	יְשׁוּעָה
אֲנִי *imperfect form from the root* ב־ט־ח, trust	—	אֶבְטַח
אֲנִי *imperfect form from the root* פ־ח־ד, be afraid	—	אֶפְחָד
strength	—	עֹז
song	—	זִמְרָת

הִנֵּה אֵל יְשׁוּעָתִי אֶבְטַח וְלֹא אֶפְחָד
כִּי עָזִּי וְזִמְרָת יָהּ יְהוָֹה וַיְהִי־לִי לִישׁוּעָה׃

5. From אֲדוֹן עוֹלָם—This passage is the last verse of a well-known hymn in praise of God, sung at the conclusion of Shabbat and holiday services.

אֲנִי *imperfect form from the root* פ־ק־ד (entrust)	—	אַפְקִיד
at the time of {when}	—	בְּעֵת
אֲנִי *imperfect form from the root* י־שׁ־ן (sleep)	—	אִישַׁן
אֲנִי *imperfect form from the root* ע־ו־ר (awaken)	—	אָעִירָה
body	—	גְּוִיָּה
אֲנִי *imperfect form from the root* י־ר־א (fear)	—	אִירָא

בְּיָדוֹ אַפְקִיד רוּחִי, בְּעֵת אִישַׁן וְאָעִירָה,
וְעִם־רוּחִי גְּוִיָּתִי, יְיָ לִי וְלֹא אִירָא.

6. Exodus 3:13–14—This passage is the continuation of Moses' encounter with God at the Burning Bush (this chapter's Torah Study Text), in which one of the more enigmatic Divine Names is revealed. The name אֶהְיֶה אֲשֶׁר אֶהְיֶה is formed from the imperfect אֲנִי form of the root ה־י־ה, "be." The translation that follows includes some of the many different ways this name has been understood.

Exodus 3:13

participle form of the root **ב־ו־א, come**	—	בָּא
אֲנִי *perfect form of the root* **א־מ־ר, say, *with reversing* vav**	—	וְאָמַרְתִּי
sent/did send/has sent	—	שָׁלַח
what	—	מָה
אֲנִי *imperfect form of the root* **א־מ־ר (say)**	—	אֹמַר

וַיֹּאמֶר מֹשֶׁה אֶל־הָאֱלֹהִים הִנֵּה אָנֹכִי בָא אֶל־בְּנֵי יִשְׂרָאֵל וְאָמַרְתִּי
לָהֶם אֱלֹהֵי אֲבוֹתֵיכֶם שְׁלָחַנִי אֲלֵיכֶם וְאָמְרוּ־לִי מַה־שְּׁמוֹ מָה
אֹמַר אֲלֵהֶם׃

Exodus 3:14

thus	—	כֹּה
you shall/will/may say	—	תֹּאמַר
sent/did send/has sent	—	שָׁלַח

וַיֹּאמֶר אֱלֹהִים אֶל־מֹשֶׁה אֶהְיֶה אֲשֶׁר אֶהְיֶה וַיֹּאמֶר כֹּה תֹאמַר
לִבְנֵי יִשְׂרָאֵל אֶהְיֶה שְׁלָחַנִי אֲלֵיכֶם׃

Translations

1. Psalm 23:1—A song of/for David. The Eternal is my shepherd; I shall/will not lack/be wanting {*or* let me not lack/be wanting *or* may I not lack/be wanting}.
2. כִּי אֶשְׁמְרָה שַׁבָּת—Because I will/shall/may keep Shabbat, God will/shall {*or* may God} keep/guard/preserve me. It is a sign for ever between Him {God} and me.
3. From Psalm 121:1–2—I shall/will {*or* May I *or* Let me} lift up my eyes to/toward the mountains, from where will/shall/may come my help/assistance. My help/assistance is from the Eternal, Maker of heaven and earth.
4. From *Havdalah* (Isaiah 12:2)—Behold, God is my salvation, I shall/will {*or* let me *or* may I} trust and not be afraid. For my strength and song is *Yah*, the Eternal, and He was/has been to/for me [for] salvation.
5. From אֲדוֹן עוֹלָם—In His {God's} hand, I shall/will {*or* let me *or* may I} entrust my spirit, at the time of {when} I shall/will/may sleep and awaken. And with my spirit, my body; the Eternal is for {with} me, and I shall/will not fear {*or* let me not fear *or* may I not fear}.
6. Exodus 3:13—Moses said to God, Behold/Here I am coming to the Children of Israel {Israelites} and I will/shall/may say to them: the God of your fathers/ancestors sent/did send/has sent me to you.

   And they will/shall/may say to me: what is His {God's} name? What shall/will/may I say to them?

   Exodus 3:14—And God said to Moses, I will/shall/may be {*or* May I be *or* Let me be} who/that/which I will/shall/may be. And he said, thus you shall/will/may say to the Children of Israel {Israelites}: I will/shall/may be sent/did send/has sent me to you.

Various Translations of אֶהְיֶה אֲשֶׁר אֶהְיֶה

I Shall Be As I Shall Be.

The Chumash, ArtScroll Series, Stone Edition. Brooklyn: Mesorah Publications,1993.

I will be-there howsoever I will be-there.

The Five Books of Moses: A New Translation with Introductions, Commentary, and Notes by Everett Fox. New York: Schocken Books, 1995.

I will ever be what I now am.

The Jerusalem Bible, published for the Nahum Zeev Williams Family Foundation at Hechal Shlomo, Jerusalem. Jerusalem: Koren Publishers Jerusalem Ltd., 1969.

Exercises

1. Read and translate the following groups of words.

a. לִבִּי ____________

בְּלִבִּי ____________

בְּלִבֵּנוּ ____________

בְּכָל לְבָבְךָ ____________

לְבָבִי ____________

b. אֲדוֹנִי ____________

אֲדוֹנֵנוּ ____________

אֲדוֹנַי ____________

אֲדוֹנֵינוּ ____________

אֲדוֹנֵיכֶם ____________

c. צְדָקָה וָחֶסֶד ____________

צִדְקָתוֹ ____________

צִדְקָתִי ____________

צִדְקוֹתֶיךָ ____________

צִדְקוֹתַי ____________

d. נִשְׁמַת חַיִּים ____________

נִשְׁמַת אָדָם ____________

נִשְׁמָתִי ____________

נִשְׁמוֹתַי ____________

נִשְׁמוֹתֵיהֶם ____________

e. רַחֲמִים רַבִּים ____________

חֶסֶד וְרַחֲמִים ____________

רַחֲמָיו ____________

רַחֲמַי ____________

בְּרַחֲמֵי הָרַבִּים ____________

f. גְּבוּרָתִי ____________

גְּבוּרָתְךָ ____________

גְּבוּרָתָהּ ____________

גְּבוּרוֹתַי ____________

גְּבוּרוֹת עַמִּי ____________

2. Identify the root of each of the following verbs and whether it is a perfect or imperfect form. Translate.

Translation	Form	Root	Verb
____________	____________	____________	אָבוֹא
____________	____________	____________	בָּחַרְתִּי
____________	____________	____________	עָבַדְתִּי
____________	____________	____________	אֶבְנֶה

Translation	Form	Root	Verb
			אֶהְיֶה
			אֲבָרֵךְ
			מָלַכְתִּי
			שָׁמַרְתִּי
			יָדַעְתִּי
			יָרֵאתִי
			אֶרְאֶה
			אֲהַלֵּל
			קִדַּשְׁתִּי
			עָשִׂיתִי
			אוֹצִיא
			הוֹצֵאתִי

3. Read and translate the following groups of sentences. Remember the use of the reversing *vav* prefix. Check your translations against those that follow.

a. מִי רָאָה אוֹר כַּזֶּה וּמִי שָׁמַע דְּבָרִים כָּאֵלֶּה? ______________

____

____

וַיַּרְא הַכֹּהֵן אֶת הָאוֹר וַיִּשְׁמַע אֶת הַקּוֹל הַהוּא. ______________

____

____

אֲנִי רָאִיתִי אֶת הָאֵשׁ וְאָז יָרֵאתִי. ______________

____

שָׁמַעְתִּי אֶת קוֹל רֵעִי בְּתוֹךְ בֵּיתִי. ______________

____

b. וַיָּבוֹאוּ בְּנֵי יִשְׂרָאֵל מִתּוֹךְ הַמִּדְבָּר וַיַּעֲלוּ אֶל אֶרֶץ כְּנָעַן. ________

וַיָּבוֹא עַמִּי עַד הַיָּם וַיֵּשְׁבוּ אַחַי וְרֵעַי בַּמָּקוֹם הַהוּא. ________

אָבוֹא עִם זַרְעִי וְשָׁם אֵשֵׁב בְּתוֹךְ הָעִיר הַזֹּאת. ________

וְהֵבֵאתִי רְפוּאָה וּגְבוּרָה וּמַעֲשֵׂי חֲסָדִים לְכָל הַחוֹלִים. ________

c. יִצְחָק לָקַח אֶת רִבְקָה לוֹ לְאִשָּׁה כִּי אָהַב אֹתָהּ. ________

לָקַחְתִּי אֶת שָׂרָה לִי לְאִשָּׁה כִּי אָהַבְתִּי אֹתָהּ. ________

וְאָהַבְתִּי אֶת אִשְׁתִּי אַחַר שָׁנִים אֲחָדוֹת וְאַחַר שָׁנִים רַבּוֹת. ________

אֶאֱהַב וַאֲהַלֵּל אֹתָהּ עַד עוֹלָם. ________

d. אַחַר הַחֹשֶׁךְ יָבוֹא הָאוֹר וְאַחַר הַלַּיְלָה יָבוֹא הַבֹּקֶר. ________

יֵשׁ נֵר אֶחָד בְּתוֹךְ הַחֹשֶׁךְ הַגָּדוֹל הַזֶּה. ________

יָדַעְתִּי כִּי יֵשׁ נָבִיא וּמוֹשִׁיעַ בְּתוֹךְ יִשְׂרָאֵל. ________

יָדַעְתִּי כִּי מִתּוֹךְ צִיּוֹן תֵּצֵא תוֹרָה וּדְבַר אֱלֹהֵינוּ מִירוּשָׁלָיִם. ________

e. אֶבְנֶה אֶת בֵּיתִי עַל רֹאשׁ הֶהָרִים בֵּין הָעֵצִים. ________

אֲבָרֵךְ אֶת בָּנַי וּפְנֵיהֶם יְבָרְכוּ אֹתִי. ________

פְּנֵי מִשְׁפַּחְתִּי יְבָרְכוּנִי כָּל יְמֵי חַיַּי. ________

מִתּוֹךְ פְּנֵיהֶם רָאִיתִי אֶת פְּנֵי אֱלֹהִים. ________

Translations

a. Who saw/was seeing/has seen/had seen a light like this and who heard/was hearing/has heard/had heard words like these?

The priest saw/did see/was seeing the light and he heard/did hear/was hearing that voice/sound.

I saw/did see/was seeing/have seen/had seen the fire and then {at that time} I was afraid/feared/did fear/had feared {was in awe/awestruck}.

I heard the voice/sound of my friend/companion/fellow/neighbor within {in the midst of} my house.

b. The Children of Israel {Israelites} came/did come/were coming out of {from the midst of} the wilderness/desert and they went up/did go up/were going up {ascended/did ascend/were ascending} to the land of Canaan.

My people/nation came/did come as far as the sea and my brothers and my friends settled/did settle {dwelt/did dwell} in that place.

I will come {Let me come/May I come} with my offspring and there I will dwell/settle {let me dwell/settle, may I dwell/settle} in the midst of {within} this city.

And I will bring {Let me bring/May I bring} healing and strength and deeds/acts of kindness to/for all the sick/ill.

c. Isaac took/did take/has taken/had taken Rebekah for/to him(self) for a wife because he loved/did love/was loving her.

I took/did take/have taken/had taken Sarah for/to me for a wife because I loved/did love/was loving her.

I will love {May I love/Let me love} my wife after a few/some years and after many years.

I will love {May I love/Let me love} and I will praise {may I praise/let me praise} her until eternity {forever}.

d. After the darkness will/may come the light {let the light come} and after the night will/may come the morning {let the morning come}.

There is one candle/lamp/light in the midst of this great darkness.

I knew/did know/had known/have known that there is a prophet and a savior in the midst of Israel.

I knew/did know/had known/have known that from the midst of Zion will/shall/may go forth Torah and the word of our God from Jerusalem.

e. I will/shall build {Let me/May I build} my house on the top of the mountains between/among the trees.

I will/shall bless {Let me/May I bless} my children and their faces will/shall bless me {let/may their faces bless me}.

The faces of my family will/shall bless me {May/Let the faces of my family bless me} all the days of my life.

From the midst of/from within their faces I have seen the face of God.

FROM OUR TEXTS

"Ani Maamin"

"Ani Maamin" is a song based on the twelfth of Maimonides' Thirteen Principles of Faith: the belief in the coming of the Messiah and, hence, in the ultimate redemption of all humankind. It is said that this song was sung by devout Jews during World War II as they faced death at the hands of the Nazis.

The new root ב־ו־א appears in the phrase בִּיאַת הַמָּשִׁיחַ, "the coming of the Messiah." An imperfect הוּא form of this root also appears in the last line: יָבוֹא, "he may come." (In this song, "he" refers to the Messiah, who traditionally was assumed to be male.) An imperfect אֲנִי form of the root ח־כ־ה ("await," "wait for") also appears.

I believe with complete faith	אֲנִי מַאֲמִין בֶּאֱמוּנָה שְׁלֵמָה
in the coming of the Messiah.	בְּבִיאַת הַמָּשִׁיחַ,
And even though he may tarry,	וְאַף עַל פִּי שֶׁיִּתְמַהְמֵהַּ,
with all this I will wait for him	עִם כָּל זֶה אֲחַכֶּה לוֹ
with every day that he may come.	בְּכָל־יוֹם שֶׁיָּבוֹא.

Torah Study Text: Leviticus 19:1–4, 15–17, 33–34

Leviticus 19 is known as the "Holiness Code," as it exhorts us to emulate the holiness of God in matters both ethical and ritual. Much of the chapter deals with relations between human beings. Excerpts from this chapter are read in Reform synagogues on the afternoon of Yom Kippur.

Read the Hebrew below to see how many of the words you can recognize. This passage does contain words, Hebrew roots, and grammatical concepts that have not yet been introduced. Underline or circle the words, roots, endings, and prefixes that you know.

Leviticus 19:1–4

1 וַיְדַבֵּר יְהוָה אֶל־מֹשֶׁה לֵּאמֹר: 2 דַּבֵּר אֶל־כָּל־עֲדַת בְּנֵי־יִשְׂרָאֵל
וְאָמַרְתָּ אֲלֵהֶם קְדֹשִׁים תִּהְיוּ כִּי קָדוֹשׁ אֲנִי יְהוָה אֱלֹהֵיכֶם: 3 אִישׁ
אִמּוֹ וְאָבִיו תִּירָאוּ וְאֶת־שַׁבְּתֹתַי תִּשְׁמֹרוּ אֲנִי יְהוָה אֱלֹהֵיכֶם:
4 אַל־תִּפְנוּ אֶל־הָאֱלִילִם וֵאלֹהֵי מַסֵּכָה לֹא תַעֲשׂוּ לָכֶם אֲנִי יְהוָה
אֱלֹהֵיכֶם:

Leviticus 19:15–17

15 לֹא־תַעֲשׂוּ עָוֶל בַּמִּשְׁפָּט לֹא־תִשָּׂא פְנֵי־דָל וְלֹא תֶהְדַּר פְּנֵי גָדוֹל
בְּצֶדֶק תִּשְׁפֹּט עֲמִיתֶךָ: 16 לֹא־תֵלֵךְ רָכִיל בְּעַמֶּיךָ לֹא תַעֲמֹד עַל־דַּם
רֵעֶךָ אֲנִי יְהוָה: 17 לֹא־תִשְׂנָא אֶת־אָחִיךָ בִּלְבָבֶךָ הוֹכֵחַ תּוֹכִיחַ
אֶת־עֲמִיתֶךָ וְלֹא־תִשָּׂא עָלָיו חֵטְא:

Leviticus 19:33–34

33 וְכִי־יָגוּר אִתְּךָ גֵּר בְּאַרְצְכֶם לֹא תוֹנוּ אֹתוֹ: 34 כְּאֶזְרָח מִכֶּם יִהְיֶה
לָכֶם הַגֵּר הַגָּר אִתְּכֶם וְאָהַבְתָּ לוֹ כָּמוֹךָ כִּי־גֵרִים הֱיִיתֶם בְּאֶרֶץ
מִצְרָיִם אֲנִי יְהוָה אֱלֹהֵיכֶם:

Translating the Torah Study Text

Following is our Torah Study Text, Leviticus 19:1–4, 15–17, 33–34, reprinted with a literal translation underneath each word. Using your knowledge of the building blocks of the Hebrew language and the meanings of the words provided below, translate this passage into clear English sentences. Write your translation on the lines following the text. This selection includes some grammatical forms and vocabulary that have not yet been introduced. You will need to rely, in part, on the translations provided.

Leviticus 19:1–4

וַיְדַבֵּר	יְהוָֹה	אֶל־	מֹשֶׁה	לֵּאמֹר:	דַּבֵּר	אֶל־	כָּל־	עֲדַת
and spoke	*the Eternal*	*to*	*Moses*	*saying*	*speak*	*to*	*all*	*congregation of*

בְּנֵי־	יִשְׂרָאֵל	וְאָמַרְתָּ	אֲלֵהֶם	קְדֹשִׁים	תִּהְיוּ	כִּי	קָדוֹשׁ
children of	*Israel*	*and say*	*to them*	*holy*	*be*	*because/ for*	*holy*

אֲנִי	יְהוָֹה	אֱלֹהֵיכֶם:	אִישׁ	אִמּוֹ	וְאָבִיו	תִּירָאוּ
I	*the Eternal*	*your God*	*(each) man*	*his mother*	*and his father*	*fear/revere*

וְאֶת־	שַׁבְּתֹתַי	תִּשְׁמֹרוּ	אֲנִי	יְהוָֹה	אֱלֹהֵיכֶם:	אַל־	תִּפְנוּ
and	*my Sabbaths*	*keep*	*I*	*the Eternal*	*your God*	*not*	*turn*

אֶל־	הָאֱלִילִם	וֵאלֹהֵי	מַסֵּכָה	לֹא	תַעֲשׂוּ	לָכֶם
to	*the idols*	*and gods of*	*molten metal*	*not*	*make*	*for you/for yourselves*

אֲנִי	יְהוָֹה	אֱלֹהֵיכֶם:
I	*the Eternal*	*your God*

Leviticus 19:15–17

דָל	פְנֵי־	תִשָּׂא	לֹא־	בַּמִּשְׁפָּט	עָוֶל	תַעֲשׂוּ	לֹא־
poor	*face of*	*lift*	*not*	*in justice/law*	*injustice/ unrighteousness*	*do*	*not*

עֲמִיתֶךָ׃	תִשְׁפֹּט	בְּצֶדֶק	גָדוֹל	פְּנֵי	תֶהְדַּר	וְלֹא
your fellow/ kinsman	*judge*	*with righteousness/ justice*	*great*	*face of*	*honor*	*and not*

רֵעֶךָ	דַּם	עַל־	תַעֲמֹד	לֹא	בְּעַמֶּיךָ	רָכִיל	תֵלֵךְ	לֹא־
your neighbor	*blood*	*on*	*stand*	*not*	*in your people*	*talebearer/ slanderer*	*go*	*not*

הוֹכֵחַ	בִּלְבָבֶךָ	אֶת־אָחִיךָ	תִשְׂנָא	לֹא־	יְהוָה׃	אֲנִי
reprove/rebuke (emphasis)	*in your heart*	*your brother*	*hate*	*not*	*the Eternal*	*I*

חֵטְא׃	עָלָיו	תִשָּׂא	וְלֹא־	עֲמִיתֶךָ	אֶת־	תּוֹכִיחַ
sin	*on (account of) him*	*bear/ carry*	*and not*	*your fellow/ kinsman*		*reprove/ rebuke*

Leviticus 19:33–34

לֹא	בְּאַרְצְכֶם	גֵּר	אִתְּךָ	יָגוּר	וְכִי־
not	*in your land*	*stranger/ sojourner*	*with you*	*may dwell/ sojourn*	*and if/ when*

תוֹנוּ	אֹתוֹ:	כְּאֶזְרָח	מִכֶּם	יִהְיֶה	לָכֶם	הַגֵּר
maltreat	*him*	*like a native*	*from you*	*shall be*	*to you*	*the stranger/ sojourner*

הַגָּר	אִתְּכֶם	וְאָהַבְתָּ	לוֹ	כָּמוֹךָ	כִּי־
who dwells/ sojourns	*with you*	*and you shall love*	*him*	*like you/ yourself*	*because/ for*

גֵרִים	הֱיִיתֶם	בְּאֶרֶץ	מִצְרָיִם	אֲנִי	יְהוָֹה	אֱלֹהֵיכֶם:
strangers/ sojourners	*you were*	*in the land of*	*Egypt*	*I*	*the Eternal*	*your God*

TORAH Translations

Compare your translation of Leviticus 19:1–4, 15–17, 33–34 with the Torah translations below.

[1]The LORD spoke to Moses, saying: [2]Speak to the whole Israelite communi-
ty and say to them:
You shall be holy, for I, the LORD your God, am holy.
[3]You shall each revere his mother and his father, and keep My sabbaths: I the LORD
am your God.
[4]Do not turn to idols or make molten gods for yourselves: I the LORD am your God....

[15]You shall not render an unfair decision: do not favor the poor or show deference to
the rich; judge your kinsman fairly. [16]Do not deal basely with your countrymen. Do not
profit by the blood of your fellow: I am the LORD.
[17]You shall not hate your kinsfolk in your heart. Reprove your kinsman but incur no
guilt because of him....

[33]When a stranger resides with you in your land, you shall not wrong him. [34]The
stranger who resides with you shall be to you as one of your citizens; you shall love
him as yourself, for you were strangers in the land of Egypt: I the LORD am your God.

JPS HEBREW-ENGLISH TANAKH: THE TRADITIONAL HEBREW TEXT AND THE NEW JPS TRANSLATION—2D ED. PHILADELPHIA: JEWISH PUBLICATION SOCIETY, 1999.

[1]HASHEM spoke to Moses, saying: [2]Speak to the entire assembly of the Children of Israel
and say to them: You shall be holy, for holy am I, HASHEM, your God.
[3]Every man: Your mother and father shall you revere and My Sabbaths shall you
observe—I am HASHEM, your God. [4]Do not turn to the idols, and molten gods shall you
not make for yourselves—I am HASHEM, your God....

[15]You shall not commit a perversion of justice; you shall not favor the poor and you
shall not honor the great; with righteousness shall you judge your fellow.
[16]You shall not be a gossipmonger among your people, you shall not stand aside
while your fellow's blood is shed—I am HASHEM. [17]You shall not hate your brother in
your heart; you shall reprove your fellow and do not bear a sin because of him....

[33]When a proselyte dwells among you in your land, do not taunt him. [34]The proselyte
who dwells with you shall be like a native among you, and you shall love him like
yourself, for you were aliens in the land of Egypt—I am HASHEM, your God.

THE CHUMASH, ARTSCROLL SERIES, STONE EDITION. BROOKLYN: MESORAH PUBLICATIONS, 1993.

[1]YHWH spoke to Moses, saying:
[2]Speak to the entire community of the Children of Israel, and say to them:
Holy are you to be,
for holy am I, YHWH your God!
[3]Each-man—his mother and his father you are to hold-in-awe,
and my Sabbaths you are to keep:
I am YHWH your God!
[4]Do not turn-your-faces to no-gods,
and molten gods you are not to make yourselves,
I am YHWH your God!...

[15]You are not to commit corruption in justice;
you are not to lift-up-in-favor the face of the poor,
you are not to overly-honor the face of the great;
with equity you are to judge your fellow!
[16]You are not to traffic in slander among your kinspeople.
You are not to stand by the blood of your neighbor,
I am YHWH!
[17]You are not to hate your brother in your heart;
rebuke, yes, rebuke your fellow,
that you not bear sin because of him!...

[33]*Now when there sojourns with you a sojourner in your land,*
you are not to maltreat him;
[34]*like the native-born among you shall he be to you, the sojourner that sojourns with you;*
be-loving to him (as one) like yourself,
for sojourners were you in the land of Egypt.
I am YHWH your God!

THE FIVE BOOKS OF MOSES: A NEW TRANSLATION WITH INTRODUCTIONS, COMMENTARY, AND NOTES BY EVERETT FOX. NEW YORK: SCHOCKEN BOOKS, 1995.

And the LORD spoke to Moshe, saying: Speak to all the congregation of the children of Yisra'el, and say to them, You shall be holy: for I the LORD your GOD am holy. You shall fear every man his mother, and his father, and keep my sabbaths: I am the LORD your GOD. Turn not to idols, nor make to yourselves molten gods: I am the LORD your GOD.

You shall do no unrighteousness in judgment: thou shalt not respect the person of the poor, nor honour the person of the mighty: but in righteousness shalt thou judge thy neighbour. Thou shalt not go up and down as a talebearer among thy people: neither shalt thou stand aside when mischief befalls thy neighbor: I am the LORD. Thou shalt not hate thy brother in thy heart: thou shalt certainly rebuke thy neighbor, and not suffer sin on his account.

And if a stranger sojourn with thee in your land, you shall not wrong him. But the stranger that dwells with you shall be to you as one born among you, and thou shalt love him as thyself; for you were strangers in the land of Mizrayim: I am the LORD your GOD.

THE JERUSALEM BIBLE, PUBLISHED FOR THE NAHUM ZEEV WILLIAMS FAMILY FOUNDATION AT HECHAL SHLOMO, JERUSALEM. JERUSALEM: KOREN PUBLISHERS JERUSALEM LTD., 1969.

Vocabulary

Locate each of the following words in the Torah Study Text: Leviticus 19:1–4, 15–17, 33–34.

saying	—	לֵאמֹר
justice, judgment, law ***m***	—	מִשְׁפָּט
stranger, sojourner ***m***	—	גֵּר
congregation, assembly, community ***f***	—	עֵדָה
no, not, don't	—	אַל
sin ***m***	—	חֵטְא

Notes on the Vocabulary

1. The word לֵאמֹר generally introduces spoken words, as in verse 1 of our Torah Study Text.
2. The word גֵּר refers to a sojourner or alien dwelling in the midst of another people. In postbiblical Hebrew, the word became used for proselytes or converts to Judaism, often in the phrase גֵּר צֶדֶק ("sincere proselyte," *literally:* "a *ger* of righteousness").
3. Unlike the negation לֹא, that can appear before verbs, adjectives, prepositions and so forth, the negation אַל is used almost exclusively before imperfect verbs, often indicating a negative command: "Don't..."

The root נ־שׂ־א appears in the פָּעַל pattern with the basic meaning of "lift," "bear," or "carry." The sounds represented by first root letter נ and the last root letter א cause variations in some of the forms. The participle, perfect, and imperfect forms are all listed in the verb charts in the back of the book.

The root נ־שׂ־א is used in idiomatic expressions such as נ־שׂ־א פָּנִים ("discriminate in favor of," "show favor to," "be partial to"), which appears in this chapter's Torah Study Text in verse 15. This root also appears in verse 17. The first root letter נ drops out in many words formed from this root.

(verse 15)

you shall not discriminate in favor of [the] poor (*literally:* you shall not lift [the] face of [the] poor)	—	לֹא־תִשָּׂא פְנֵי־דָל

(verse 17)

and you shall not bear/carry on (account of) him sin	—	וְלֹא־תִשָּׂא עָלָיו חֵטְא

The following words and expressions, both ancient and modern, are derived from the root נ־שׂ־א. The first root letter נ drops out in many words formed from this root.

chief, prince; president	—	נָשִׂיא
load, burden; utterance, oracle	—	מַשָּׂא
negotiations, trade, bargaining *(give and take)*	—	מַשָּׂא־וּמַתָּן
longing, yearning, aspiration	—	מַשָּׂא נֶפֶשׁ
lifting; rising smoke; yearning, desire	—	מַשָּׂאָה
truck	—	מַשָּׂאִית
beacon, signal light	—	מַשּׂוּאָה
exaltation, dignity; bearing, endurance	—	שְׂאֵת
high, lofty, exalted	—	נִשָּׂא
wedding, marriage	—	נִשּׂוּאִין
married	—	נָשׂוּי
carrying, bearing, transportation	—	נְשִׂיאָה
favoritism, bias, partiality	—	נְשִׂיאַת פָּנִים

The root ע־מ־ד appears in the פָּעַל pattern with the basic meaning "stand." In the הִפְעִיל pattern, it means "cause to stand," "erect," "set up," or "establish." The participle, perfect, and imperfect forms of the root ע־מ־ד in both the פָּעַל and הִפְעִיל patterns can be found in the verb charts in the back of the book.

The root ע־מ־ד appears once in our Torah Study Text:

(verse 16)

you shall not stand on {by} the blood of your neighbor	—	לֹא תַעֲמֹד עַל־דַּם רֵעֶךָ

The following words and expressions, both ancient and modern, are derived from the root ע־מ־ד.

standing-place, post, platform	—	עֹמֶד
position, standpoint	—	עֶמְדָּה

pillar, column; page	—	עַמּוּד
class, standing, position, status	—	מַעֲמָד
the revelation at Mount Sinai	—	מַעֲמַד הַר סִינַי
candidate, nominee	—	מֻעֲמָד
resistant, withstanding	—	עָמִיד
waterproof	—	עֲמִיד־מַיִם
standing; *also* the name of the unit of prayers that forms the core of weekday, Shabbat, and holiday services, traditionally said standing	—	עֲמִידָה

The following phrase is used in synagogue for calling someone up to the בִּימָה ("lectern") for an עֲלִיָּה—the honor of saying the blessings before and after the Torah reading:

Let X *(Hebrew name)* the daughter of X *(parents' Hebrew names)* stand	—	תַּעֲמֹד X בַּת X
Let X *(Hebrew name)* the son of X *(parents' Hebrew names)* stand	—	יַעֲמֹד X בֶּן X

TORAH Commentary

The phrase אֲנִי יְהוָה אֱלֹהֵיכֶם, "I am the Eternal your God," is repeated at the end of verses 2, 3, and 4. What can we learn from this seemingly unnecessary repetition?

Rabbi Avraham Abele of Vilna asked, why does each sentence end with "I am your G-d!" Could not all three verses have been combined, and the closing phrase, "I am your G-d," applied to all three? And he answers that the Torah wishes to indicate that while there may be various levels of spirituality and Torah observance, no Jew loses his relationship with G-d. G-d remains in contact with everyone.

The highest level is the person who lives a life of kedushah *(holiness), and to whom G-d says, "I am your G-d." At a lesser level is the person who may not have achieved* kedushah, *but who observes the fundamental* mitzvos, *which are represented by the commandment to revere one's parents and to observe Shabbos. To this person G-d also says, "Even if you have not achieved the highest level, nevertheless, I am your G-d." And finally, even to a person who has failed to observe the* mitzvos, *but rejects idolatry and has a rudimentary belief in G-d, to him G-d also says, "I am your G-d."*

RABBI ABRAHAM J. TWERSKI M.D., *LIVING EACH WEEK.* BROOKLYN: MESORAH PUBLICATIONS LTD., 1992.

In verse 15, the phrase לֹא־תַעֲשׂוּ עָוֶל בַּמִּשְׁפָּט, "you shall not do injustice/unrighteousness in justice/judgment/law," is generally understood to mean, as implied by the context, that laws should not be unfairly applied. The following simple commentary, however, gives the same phrase a much broader social implication.

> ***You shall do no unrighteousness in judgement...*** *Do not legalize injustice by means of [unjust] judgments and laws.*
>
> R. Simchah Bunim of Pshischa as quoted in *Torah Gems*, comp. Aharon Yaakov Greenberg, trans. R. Dr. Shmuel Himelstein. Tel Aviv and Brooklyn: Yavneh Publishing House, Chemed Books, 1998.

In verse 17, the phrase לֹא־תִשְׂנָא אֶת־אָחִיךָ בִּלְבָבֶךָ, "you shall not hate your brother in your heart," is followed by the statement הוֹכֵחַ תּוֹכִיחַ אֶת־עֲמִיתֶךָ וְלֹא־תִשָּׂא עָלָיו חֵטְא, "you shall (*emphasis*) reprove/rebuke your fellow/kinsman and you shall not bear/carry on (account of) him sin." What is the connection between the first and the second part of the verse?

> *One who wishes to rebuke another must first examine whether he holds any personal grudge against the other person. Only if you are sure that you do not hate your neighbor in your heart are you permitted to rebuke your neighbor.*
>
> R. Yehudah Leib, the Mokhi'ach of Polonnoye, as quoted in *Torah Gems*, comp. Aharon Yaakov Greenberg, trans. by R. Dr. Shmuel Himelstein. Tel Aviv and Brooklyn: Yavneh Publishing House, Chemed Books, 1998.

Verses 33–34 command us not to wrong the stranger who dwells in our midst because we were strangers in the land of Egypt. Rashi draws a lesson from this idea and from the use of the plural ending כֶם on the word אֱלֹהֵיכֶם, "your God," that concludes verse 34.

> כִּי־גֵרִים הֱיִיתֶם, ***for you were strangers.*** *Do not criticize your neighbor for a fault that also exists in yourself.* אֲנִי יְהוָֹה אֱלֹהֵיכֶם, ***I am the Eternal your*** (plural) ***God.*** *I am your God and his God. (I am the God of both of you.)*
>
> Rashi on Leviticus 19:33–34

Exercises

1. Make flash cards for each of the new vocabulary words and Hebrew roots introduced in this chapter, or use the flash card set published as a companion to this book. Review the cards to learn all of them.

2. Draw a line connecting each Hebrew word to its English translation. For some words, there can be more than one correct translation.

law	עֵדָה
not	
congregation	גֵּר
saying	
stranger	לֵאמֹר
community	חֵטְא
sin	
sojourner	אַל
no	
justice	מִשְׁפָּט

3. On the left are plural forms of words introduced as vocabulary in this chapter. Draw a line connecting each plural word to its singular form. Translate both into English.

________________	מִשְׁפָּטִים	חֵטְא	________________
________________	חֲטָאִים	גֵּר	________________
________________	עֵדוֹת	מִשְׁפָּט	________________
________________	גֵּרִים	עֵדָה	________________

4. Read and translate the following groups of words.

a. בְּתוֹךְ הָעֵדָה ______

______

בְּעֵינֵי הָעֵדָה ______

______

עֲדַת יִשְׂרָאֵל ______

______

עֲדַת אֵל ______

עֲדָתִי ______

b. אֱמֶת וּמִשְׁפָּט ______

______

מִשְׁפָּט וָצֶדֶק ______

רוּחַ מִשְׁפָּט ______

______

שׁוֹמְרֵי מִשְׁפָּט ______

______

מְקוֹם הַמִּשְׁפָּט ______

______

c. חֲטָאִים גְּדוֹלִים ______

______

חֲטָאַי ______

חֲטָאָיו ______

חֲטָאֵינוּ ______

חֲטָאֵיכֶם ______

d. נֶפֶשׁ הַגֵּר ______

מִשְׁפַּט גֵּר ______

אִישׁ גֵּר ______

גֵּרְךָ ______

כְּגֵר בָּאָרֶץ ______

e. וַיְבָרֶךְ אֹתָם אֱלֹהִים לֵאמֹר... ______

______

וַיְצַו הַמֶּלֶךְ אֶת הָעֶבֶד לֵאמֹר... ______

______

וַיֹּאמֶר אֱלֹהִים אֶל־יַעֲקֹב לֵאמֹר... ______

______

וַיְדַבֵּר עִם הָאָדָם לֵאמֹר... ______

______

וַיְהִי דְבַר־יְיָ אֵלַי לֵאמֹר... ______

5. Identify the root of each of the following verbs and whether it is a perfect, imperfect, or participle form. Translate.

Translation	Form	Root	Verb
			נוֹשֵׂא
			עוֹמֶדֶת
			רוֹאוֹת
			תָּבוֹא
			יַעַמְדוּ
			אֶעֱבֹד
			אֶהְיֶה
			יָדַעְתִּי
			הָלַכְתִּי
			נָשָׂאתִי
			יָרֵאתִי
			מַעֲמִידִים

EXTRA CREDIT

All the Rest Is Commentary

In verse 34 of this chapter's Torah Study Text, we read:

כְּאֶזְרָח מִכֶּם יִהְיֶה לָכֶם הַגֵּר הַגָּר אִתְּכֶם וְאָהַבְתָּ לוֹ כָּמוֹךָ...

"Like a native among you shall be the stranger/sojourner who dwells with you and you shall love him {that person} as yourself...."

A broader version of this idea, applying not only to strangers but to everyone with whom we interact, is found in Leviticus 19:18, also part of the Holiness Code: וְאָהַבְתָּ לְרֵעֲךָ כָּמוֹךָ, "Love your neighbor/friend/companion/fellow as yourself."

The Golden Rule, "Do unto others as you would have others do unto you," is a variation on the same idea, as is the following version attributed to the famous rabbinic sage Hillel, related in the Talmud, *Shabbat* 31a.

> *It happened that a certain heathen came before Shammai and said to him, "Make me a proselyte, on condition that you teach me the whole Torah while I stand on one foot." Thereupon he [Shammai] repulsed him (chased him off) with the builder's tool (builder's measure, cubit) that was in his hand. When he went before Hillel, he [Hillel] said to him, "What is hateful to you, do not do to your neighbor. That is the whole Torah. All the rest is commentary. Now go and learn (study it)."*

Hillel's statement that all the rest is commentary does not mean that the rest of Jewish law is insignificant. In the Talmud, much of the text is commentary, surrounding and elaborating on a central idea.

On the right is a reproduction of the page of the Talmud on which the narrative above appears. As you can see, there is much commentary surrounding the central text. This commentary is an essential part of the learning. Hillel's remark does not conclude with the statement "All the rest is commentary" as if to dismiss the commentary, but with the exhortation "Now go and learn." A thorough knowledge of Jewish law can guide us in fulfilling the essential idea of loving others as ourselves.

Torah Study Text: Vocabulary and Root Review

This unit's Torah Study Text, Leviticus 19:1–4, 15–17, 33–34, is reprinted below, highlighting the new vocabulary words as well as the words formed from the new Hebrew roots introduced in Chapter 5. Read this passage again, recalling the meaning of each of the highlighted words or roots.

Leviticus 19:1–4

1 וַיְדַבֵּר יְהוָֹה אֶל־מֹשֶׁה **לֵּאמֹר**׃ 2 דַּבֵּר אֶל־כָּל־**עֲדַת** בְּנֵי־יִשְׂרָאֵל
וְאָמַרְתָּ אֲלֵהֶם קְדֹשִׁים תִּהְיוּ כִּי קָדוֹשׁ אֲנִי יְהוָֹה אֱלֹהֵיכֶם׃ 3 אִישׁ
אִמּוֹ וְאָבִיו תִּירָאוּ וְאֶת־שַׁבְּתֹתַי תִּשְׁמֹרוּ אֲנִי יְהוָֹה אֱלֹהֵיכֶם׃
4 **אַל**־תִּפְנוּ אֶל־הָאֱלִילִם וֵאלֹהֵי מַסֵּכָה לֹא תַעֲשׂוּ לָכֶם אֲנִי יְהוָֹה
אֱלֹהֵיכֶם׃

Leviticus 19:15–17

15 לֹא־תַעֲשׂוּ עָוֶל **בַּמִּשְׁפָּט** לֹא־**תִשָּׂא** פְנֵי־דָל וְלֹא תֶהְדַּר פְּנֵי גָדוֹל
בְּצֶדֶק תִּשְׁפֹּט עֲמִיתֶךָ׃ 16 לֹא־תֵלֵךְ רָכִיל בְּעַמֶּיךָ לֹא **תַעֲמֹד** עַל־דַּם
רֵעֶךָ אֲנִי יְהוָֹה׃ 17 לֹא־תִשְׂנָא אֶת־אָחִיךָ בִּלְבָבֶךָ הוֹכֵחַ תּוֹכִיחַ
אֶת־עֲמִיתֶךָ וְלֹא־**תִשָּׂא** עָלָיו **חֵטְא**׃

Leviticus 19:33–34

33 וְכִי־יָגוּר אִתְּךָ **גֵּר** בְּאַרְצְכֶם לֹא תוֹנוּ אֹתוֹ׃ 34 כְּאֶזְרָח מִכֶּם יִהְיֶה
לָכֶם הַ**גֵּר** הַגָּר אִתְּכֶם וְאָהַבְתָּ לוֹ כָּמוֹךָ כִּי־**גֵרִ**ים הֱיִיתֶם בְּאֶרֶץ
מִצְרָיִם אֲנִי יְהוָֹה אֱלֹהֵיכֶם׃

Building Blocks

"You" Verb Forms

In English, the word "you" can be addressed to a single male or female or to a group of people. In Hebrew, there are four different words for "you": masculine singular, feminine singular, masculine plural, and feminine plural. The word אַתָּה, introduced in Chapter 1 of *Aleph Isn't Enough*, is a masculine singular form, used for addressing a single male.

In Hebrew, the "you" verb forms are distinctly either masculine or feminine, singular or plural, and perfect or imperfect. Because the feminine forms appear very seldom in the Bible and prayer book, we are not presenting those forms in the body of this book. They are, however, included in the verb charts in the back of the book.

Perfect Forms: The תָּ and תֶּם Endings

The ending תָּ (or, in some cases, תָ) attached to a verb indicates that the verb is a perfect אַתָּה—masculine singular "you"—form. This same ending is used with all the Hebrew verb patterns. Following are examples of פָּעַל, פִּעֵל, and הִפְעִיל verbs with this ending attached:

you loved	—	אָהַבְתָּ
you sanctified/made holy	—	קִדַּשְׁתָּ
you caused to stand/set up/ established	—	הֶעֱמַדְתָּ

Remember that perfect verbs describe action that has been completed and can be translated in several different ways. For example, אָהַבְתָּ could be translated as "you loved," "you did love," "you have loved," or "you had loved."

The ending תֶּם (or תֶם) indicates a perfect masculine plural "you" form in all the Hebrew verb patterns. Masculine plural forms are used in Hebrew both for all-male groups and for mixed-gender groups.

you *(plural)* loved	—	אֲהַבְתֶּם
you *(plural)* sanctified/made holy	—	קִדַּשְׁתֶּם
you *(plural)* caused to stand/set up/ established	—	הֶעֱמַדְתֶּם

Remember that the verbs listed above could be translated in other ways.

Imperfect Forms: The תּ Prefix and וּ Ending

The prefix תּ (or, in some cases, ת) indicates that a verb is an imperfect אַתָּה—masculine singular "you"—form. This same prefix is used with all the Hebrew verb patterns. The vowels appearing under the prefix vary, depending on the verb pattern and root letters. Following are examples of פָּעַל, פִּעֵל, and הִפְעִיל verbs with this prefix attached. Notice that the imperfect אַתָּה, "you," form is the same as the imperfect "she" form. The context determines which meaning is intended.

you will/may love — תֶּאֱהַב

you will/may sanctify/make holy — תְּקַדֵּשׁ

you will/may cause to stand/set up/ establish — תַּעֲמִיד

Remember that imperfect verbs can indicate the future tense, ongoing incompleted action, or action that is wished or urged. So, for example, תֶּאֱהַב could be translated as "you will love," "you may love," "may you love," or "you shall love."

The prefix תּ (or ת) together with the ending וּ indicate an imperfect masculine plural "you" form in all the Hebrew verb patterns. Masculine plural forms are used in Hebrew both for all-male groups and for mixed-gender groups.

you *(plural)* will/may love — תֶּאֱהָבוּ

you *(plural)* will/may sanctify/make holy — תְּקַדְּשׁוּ

you *(plural)* will/may cause to stand/set up/establish — תַּעֲמִידוּ

Remember that the verbs listed above could be translated in other ways.

Torah Study Text with Building Blocks

Following is this unit's Torah Study Text, Leviticus 19:1–4, 15–17, 33–34, reprinted with the new Building Blocks highlighted. Reread these verses, noting the appearance of singular and plural "you" perfect and imperfect verb forms. A translation is provided below for only the highlighted Building Blocks. Remember that there could be other possible translations. For a full translation of the verses, refer back to Chapter 5.

Leviticus 19:1–4

1 וַיְדַבֵּר יְהוָה אֶל־מֹשֶׁה לֵּאמֹר: 2 דַּבֵּר אֶל־כָּל־עֲדַת בְּנֵי־יִשְׂרָאֵל

וְאָמַרְתָּ אֲלֵהֶם קְדֹשִׁים **תִּהְיוּ** כִּי קָדוֹשׁ אֲנִי יְהוָה אֱלֹהֵיכֶם׃ 3 אִישׁ
אִמּוֹ וְאָבִיו **תִּירָאוּ** וְאֶת־שַׁבְּתֹתַי **תִּשְׁמֹרוּ** אֲנִי יְהוָה אֱלֹהֵיכֶם׃
4 אַל־**תִּפְנוּ** אֶל־הָאֱלִילִם וֵאלֹהֵי מַסֵּכָה לֹא **תַעֲשׂוּ** לָכֶם אֲנִי יְהוָה
אֱלֹהֵיכֶם׃

Leviticus 19:15–17

15 לֹא־**תַעֲשׂוּ** עָוֶל בַּמִּשְׁפָּט לֹא־**תִשָּׂא** פְנֵי־דָל וְלֹא **תֶהְדַּר** פְּנֵי גָדוֹל
בְּצֶדֶק **תִּשְׁפֹּט** עֲמִיתֶךָ׃ 16 לֹא־**תֵלֵךְ** רָכִיל בְּעַמֶּיךָ לֹא **תַעֲמֹד** עַל־דַּם
רֵעֶךָ אֲנִי יְהוָה׃ 17 לֹא־**תִשְׂנָא** אֶת־אָחִיךָ בִּלְבָבֶךָ הוֹכֵחַ **תּוֹכִיחַ**
אֶת־עֲמִיתֶךָ וְלֹא־**תִשָּׂא** עָלָיו חֵטְא׃

Leviticus 19:33–34

33 וְכִי־יָגוּר אִתְּךָ גֵּר בְּאַרְצְכֶם לֹא **תוֹנוּ** אֹתוֹ׃ 34 כְּאֶזְרָח מִכֶּם יִהְיֶה
לָכֶם הַגֵּר הַגָּר אִתְּכֶם **וְאָהַבְתָּ** לוֹ כָּמוֹךָ כִּי־גֵרִים **הֱיִיתֶם** בְּאֶרֶץ
מִצְרָיִם אֲנִי יְהוָה אֱלֹהֵיכֶם׃

(and) you will/shall say *(perfect form with reversing* vav *attached)*	—	וְאָמַרְתָּ
you *(plural)* will/shall be	—	תִּהְיוּ
you *(plural)* will/shall fear/revere	—	תִּירְאוּ
you *(plural)* will/shall keep	—	תִּשְׁמְרוּ
you *(plural)* will/shall turn	—	תִּפְנוּ
you *(plural)* will/shall make	—	תַּעֲשׂוּ
you will/shall lift	—	תִּשָּׂא
you will/shall honor	—	תֶּהְדַּר
you will/shall judge	—	תִּשְׁפֹּט
you will/shall go	—	תֵּלֵךְ
you will/shall stand	—	תַּעֲמֹד
you will/shall hate	—	תִּשְׂנָא
you will/shall reprove/rebuke	—	תּוֹכִיחַ

you *(plural)* will/shall maltreat	—	תּוֹנוּ
(and) you will/shall love (*perfect form with reversing* vav *attached*)	—	וְאָהַבְתָּ
you *(plural)* were	—	הֱיִיתֶם

GRAMMAR Enrichment

Perfect and Imperfect Forms for אַתָּה and אַתֶּם

The following charts include the "you" masculine singular and plural forms (אַתָּה and אַתֶּם) in the perfect and imperfect for all the roots introduced thus far in this book and in *Bet Is for B'reishit*. The פָּעַל, פִּעֵל, and הִפְעִיל verb patterns are included. These are presented for enrichment only. It is not necessary to memorize the information on these charts.

It may be helpful to notice certain variations:

- In roots that end with the letter ה, such as ב־נ־ה, ה־י־ה, ר־א־ה, ע־ל־ה, ח־י־ה, and צ־ו־ה, the root letter ה drops out in all the "you" forms except the imperfect singular. This also happens with the middle root letter ו in the perfect "you" forms for roots such as ב־ו־א.
- In many roots that begin with the letters י or נ, such as י־ד־ע, י־צ־א, י־שׁ־ב, and נ־ת־ן, that first root letter drops out in the imperfect "you" forms.

פָּעַל Verbs

Imperfect Plural	Imperfect Singular	Perfect Plural	Perfect Singular	Root	Meaning
תֹּאמְרוּ	תֹּאמַר	אֲמַרְתֶּם	אָמַרְתָּ	א־מ־ר	say
תָּבוֹאוּ	תָּבוֹא	בָּאתֶם	בָּאתָ	ב־ו־א	come
תִּבְנוּ	תִּבְנֶה	בְּנִיתֶם	בָּנִיתָ	ב־נ־ה	build
תִּהְיוּ	תִּהְיֶה	הֱיִיתֶם	הָיִיתָ	ה־י־ה	be
תֵּלְכוּ	תֵּלֵךְ	הֲלַכְתֶּם	הָלַכְתָּ	ה־ל־ך	walk, go
תֵּדְעוּ	תֵּדַע	יְדַעְתֶּם	יָדַעְתָּ	י־ד־ע	know
תִּירְאוּ	תִּירָא	יְרֵאתֶם	יָרֵאתָ	י־ר־א	fear, be in awe
תֵּשְׁבוּ	תֵּשֵׁב	יְשַׁבְתֶּם	יָשַׁבְתָּ	י־שׁ־ב	sit, dwell
תִּקְחוּ	תִּקַּח	לְקַחְתֶּם	לָקַחְתָּ	ל־ק־ח	take
תִּשְׂאוּ	תִּשָּׂא	נְשָׂאתֶם	נָשָׂאתָ	נ־שׂ־א	lift, bear, carry
תַּעַבְדוּ	תַּעֲבֹד	עֲבַדְתֶּם	עָבַדְתָּ	ע־ב־ד	work, serve

תַּעֲלוּ	תַּעֲלֶה	עֲלִיתֶם	עָלִיתָ	ע־ל־ה	go up, ascend
תַּעַמְדוּ	תַּעֲמֹד	עֲמַדְתֶּם	עָמַדְתָּ	ע־מ־ד	stand
תִּרְאוּ	תִּרְאֶה	רְאִיתֶם	רָאִיתָ	ר־א־ה	see

פִּעֵל Verbs

Imperfect Plural	Imperfect Singular	Perfect Plural	Perfect Singular	Root	Meaning
תְּבָרְכוּ	תְּבָרֵךְ	בֵּרַכְתֶּם	בֵּרַכְתָּ	ב־ר־ךְ	bless
תְּדַבְּרוּ	תְּדַבֵּר	דִּבַּרְתֶּם	דִּבַּרְתָּ	ד־ב־ר	speak, talk
תְּהַלְלוּ	תְּהַלֵּל	הִלַּלְתֶּם	הִלַּלְתָּ	ה־ל־ל	praise
תְּחַיּוּ	תְּחַיֶּה	חִיִּיתֶם	חִיִּיתָ	ח־י־ה	bring to life
תְּצַוּוּ	תְּצַוֶּה	צִוִּיתֶם	צִוִּיתָ	צ־ו־ה	command, order
תְּקַדְּשׁוּ	תְּקַדֵּשׁ	קִדַּשְׁתֶּם	קִדַּשְׁתָּ	ק־ד־שׁ	make holy

הִפְעִיל Verbs

Imperfect Plural	Imperfect Singular	Perfect Plural	Perfect Singular	Root	Meaning
תּוֹלִיכוּ	תּוֹלִיךְ	הוֹלַכְתֶּם	הוֹלַכְתָּ	ה־ל־ךְ	cause to go, lead, conduct
תַּחֲיוּ	תַּחֲיֶה	הֶחֱיִיתֶם	הֶחֱיִיתָ	ח־י־ה	keep alive
תּוֹדִיעוּ	תּוֹדִיעַ	הוֹדַעְתֶּם	הוֹדַעְתָּ	י־ד־ע	make known, announce
תּוֹצִיאוּ	תּוֹצִיא	הוֹצֵאתֶם	הוֹצֵאתָ	י־צ־א	cause to go out, bring out
תּוֹשִׁיבוּ	תּוֹשִׁיב	הוֹשַׁבְתֶּם	הוֹשַׁבְתָּ	י־שׁ־ב	cause to sit *or* dwell, seat
תַּעֲבִידוּ	תַּעֲבִיד	הֶעֱבַדְתֶּם	הֶעֱבַדְתָּ	ע־ב־ד	put to work, employ
תַּעֲלוּ	תַּעֲלֶה	הֶעֱלִיתֶם	הֶעֱלִיתָ	ע־ל־ה	cause to ascend, bring up
תַּעֲמִידוּ	תַּעֲמִיד	הֶעֱמַדְתֶּם	הֶעֱמַדְתָּ	ע־מ־ד	cause to stand, establish
תַּרְאוּ	תַּרְאֶה	הֶרְאֵיתֶם	הֶרְאֵיתָ	ר־א־ה	cause to see, show

Additional Reading and Translation Practice

Translate the following excerpts from the Bible and the prayer book, using the extra vocabulary words provided. Check your translations against the English translations that follow.

1. From Psalm 121:1–2: These verses have been set to music and are sung in some liturgical settings. The first word is an imperfect אֲנִי form from the root נ־שׂ־א.

from where	—	מֵאַיִן
help, assistance	—	עֵזֶר
from	—	מֵעִם

...אֶשָּׂא עֵינַי אֶל־הֶהָרִים מֵאַיִן יָבֹא עֶזְרִי׃
עֶזְרִי מֵעִם יְהוָה עוֹשֵׂה שָׁמַיִם וָאָרֶץ׃

____

____

2. עַל שְׁלֹשָׁה דְבָרִים: This song derived from *Mishnah Avot* 1:2 is sometimes sung as the Torah is carried from the ark. A participle form of the root ע־מ־ד appears. The word דְּבָרִים in this context means not "words," but "things."

three	—	שְׁלֹשָׁה
worship	—	הָעֲבוֹדָה
doing [acts of] kindness	—	גְּמִלוּת חֲסָדִים

עַל־שְׁלֹשָׁה דְבָרִים הָעוֹלָם עוֹמֵד: עַל הַתּוֹרָה וְעַל הָעֲבוֹדָה וְעַל גְּמִלוּת חֲסָדִים.

____

____

3. לְמַ֫עַן תִּזְכְּרוּ (Numbers 15:40–41): These biblical verses are among those said after the שְׁמַע in the morning and evening service. A plural "you" form of the root ז־כ־ר appears in the imperfect. Plural "you" forms of the roots ע־שׂ־ה and ה־י־ה appear in the perfect with reversing *vav* attached.

so that	—	לְמַ֫עַן
אֲנִי *perfect* הִפְעִיל *form from the root* י־צ־א, bring out	—	הוֹצֵאתִי
to be	—	לִהְיוֹת

לְמַ֫עַן תִּזְכְּרוּ וַעֲשִׂיתֶם אֶת־כָּל־מִצְוֹתָי, וִהְיִיתֶם קְדֹשִׁים לֵאלֹהֵיכֶם:
אֲנִי יְיָ אֱלֹהֵיכֶם, אֲשֶׁר הוֹצֵאתִי אֶתְכֶם מֵאֶ֫רֶץ מִצְרַ֫יִם לִהְיוֹת
לָכֶם לֵאלֹהִים, אֲנִי יְיָ אֱלֹהֵיכֶם:

____

____

____

4. From the most common version of the Shabbat Evening קִדּוּשׁ: This excerpt is from the blessing sanctifying the Sabbath, said over wine on Friday evening. The אַתָּה, "you," form of the roots ב־ח־ר and ק־ד־שׁ appear in the perfect. Reminder: the preposition ב is not translated "in" or "with" when accompanying the root ב־ח־ר.

love	—	אַהֲבָה
favor	—	רָצוֹן
you have bequeathed {given as an inheritance}	—	הִנְחַ֫לְתָּ
you have bequeathed us {you have given us as an inheritance}	—	הִנְחַלְתָּ֫נוּ

כִּי־בָ֫נוּ בָחַ֫רְתָּ וְאוֹתָ֫נוּ קִדַּ֫שְׁתָּ מִכָּל הָעַמִּים, וְשַׁבַּת קָדְשְׁךָ בְּאַהֲבָה
וּבְרָצוֹן הִנְחַלְתָּ֫נוּ.

____

____

5. Deuteronomy 4:39 (included in the עָלֵינוּ): The biblical verse Deuteronomy 4:39 is quoted in the עָלֵינוּ, said during the concluding section of weekday, Sabbath, and holiday services. A perfect אַתָּה, "you," form from the root י־ד־ע appears with reversing *vav* attached.

today	—	הַיּוֹם
and return/restore	—	וַהֲשֵׁבֹתָ
above	—	מִמַּעַל
below	—	מִתָּחַת
other	—	עוֹד

וְיָדַעְתָּ הַיּוֹם וַהֲשֵׁבֹתָ אֶל־לְבָבֶךָ, כִּי יְיָ הוּא הָאֱלֹהִים בַּשָּׁמַיִם
מִמַּעַל וְעַל־הָאָרֶץ מִתָּחַת, אֵין עוֹד:

6. From the בִּרְכַּת הַמָּזוֹן, the Blessing after Meals: This excerpt includes the biblical verse Deuteronomy 8:10. The אַתָּה, "you," form of the roots א־כ־ל, שׂ־ב־ע, and ב־ר־ך appear in the perfect with reversing *vav* attached.

written	—	כָּתוּב
as it is written	—	כַּכָּתוּב
***root meaning* be satisfied**	—	שׂ־ב־ע
food, nourishment, sustenance	—	הַמָּזוֹן

כַּכָּתוּב, "וְאָכַלְתָּ וְשָׂבָעְתָּ, וּבֵרַכְתָּ אֶת־יְיָ אֱלֹהֶיךָ עַל־הָאָרֶץ
הַטֹּבָה אֲשֶׁר נָתַן־לָךְ." בָּרוּךְ אַתָּה יְיָ, עַל־הָאָרֶץ וְעַל־הַמָּזוֹן.

7. Leviticus 25:10: This passage is from the biblical description of the Jubilee year. A translation of a portion of this verse is inscribed on the Liberty Bell in Philadelphia. Plural "you" forms of the roots ק־ר־א and ק־ד־ש appear in the perfect with reversing *vav* attached.

fiftieth	—	חֲמִשִּׁים
***root meaning* proclaim**	—	ק־ר־א
liberty (also, release)	—	דְּרוֹר
its inhabitants (its settlers/dwellers)— (*participle from* י־ש־ב)	—	יֹשְׁבֶיהָ

וְקִדַּשְׁתֶּם אֵת שְׁנַת הַחֲמִשִּׁים שָׁנָה וּקְרָאתֶם דְּרוֹר בָּאָרֶץ
לְכָל־יֹשְׁבֶיהָ...

Translations

1. From Psalm 121:1–2—I shall/will {*or* May I *or* Let me} lift up my eyes to/toward the mountains, from where will/shall/may come my help/assistance. My help/assistance is from the Eternal, Maker of heaven and earth.
2. עַל שְׁלֹשָׁה דְּבָרִים—Upon three things the world stands/is standing/does stand: upon the Torah, and upon worship, and upon doing [acts of] kindness.
3. לְמַעַן תִּזְכְּרוּ (Numbers 15:40–41)—So that you will/shall/may remember and you will/shall/may do all my commandments and you will/shall/may be {let/may you be} holy to your God. I, the Eternal, am your God {I am the Eternal, your God}, that I brought out you {brought you out} from the land of Egypt, to be to/for you for your God. I am the Eternal your God {I, the Eternal, am your God}.
4. From the Shabbat evening קִדּוּשׁ—For us You have chosen/chose/did choose and us You have sanctified {made holy} from all the peoples/nations, and the Sabbath of your holiness {your holy Sabbath} with love and with favor you have bequeathed us {you have given us as an inheritance}.
5. Deuteronomy 4:39 (included in the עָלֵינוּ)—And you shall/will/may know {May you know} today and return/restore to your heart, that the Eternal is the God in the heavens above and on the earth below, there is no/none other.
6. From the בִּרְכַּת הַמָּזוֹן—As it is written, "And you will/shall/may eat, be satisfied, and bless {May you eat, be satisfied, and bless} the Eternal your God about {regarding, for} the good earth/land that [God] gave/has given/did give to you." Blessed are You, Eternal One, about {regarding, for} the land/earth and about {regarding, for} the food/nourishment/sustenance.

7. Leviticus 25:10—And you will/shall sanctify {make holy} the year of the fiftieth year and you shall/will proclaim liberty in the land to all its inhabitants...

Exercises

1. Read and translate the following groups of words:

a. אַל תִּשְׁמַע ______________
אַל תִּשְׁמְעוּ ______________
אַל תִּירָא ______________
אַל תִּירְאוּ ______________
אַל תִּרְאֶה ______________

b. אַל תֹּאכְלוּ ______________
אַל תֹּאכַל ______________
אַל תָּבוֹא ______________
אַל תָּבוֹאוּ ______________
אַל תִּבְנוּ ______________

c. אַל תֵּלֵךְ ______________
אַל תֵּלְכוּ ______________
אַל תַּעֲזוֹר ______________
אַל תַּעַזְרוּ ______________
אַל תְּדַבְּרוּ ______________

2. Draw a line connecting each of the following plural "you" verb forms with the corresponding singular form. Identify the root and whether it is a perfect or imperfect form. Translate the singular form.

Translation	Form	Root	Singular	Plural
____________	________	________	עָבַדְתָּ	בָּאתֶם
____________	________	________	לָקַחְתָּ	רְאִיתֶם
____________	________	________	הָלַכְתָּ	הֱיִיתֶם
____________	________	________	תִּבְנֶה	נְשָׂאתֶם
____________	________	________	תַּעֲלֶה	תַּעַמְדוּ
____________	________	________	יָרֵאתָ	תִּירְאוּ
____________	________	________	רָאִיתָ	תִּבְנוּ
____________	________	________	תִּירָא	עֲבַדְתֶּם
____________	________	________	הָיִיתָ	הוֹשַׁבְתֶּם
____________	________	________	בָּאתָ	צִוִּיתֶם
____________	________	________	נָשָׂאתָ	תְּהַלְלוּ
____________	________	________	תַּעֲמֹד	לְקַחְתֶּם
____________	________	________	תְּהַלֵּל	יְרֵאתֶם
____________	________	________	צִוִּיתָ	הֲלַכְתֶּם
____________	________	________	הוֹשַׁבְתָּ	תַּעֲלוּ

3. Read and translate the following groups of sentences. Remember the use of the reversing *vav* prefix. Check your translations against those that follow.

a. הוּא נָשָׂא אֶת עֵינָיו וְאָז רָאָה אֶת הַדָּם עַל פְּנֵי רֵעֵהוּ. ____________

____

____

נָשָׂאתָ אֶת עֵינֶיךָ וְאָז רָאִיתָ אֶת דַּם רֵעֶךָ. ____________

____

וַיִּשָּׂא אֶת עֵינָיו וַיַּרְא וְהִנֵּה דָם עַל יָדָיו. ______________

____

____

וַתִּשְׂאוּ אֶת עֵינֵיכֶם וַתִּרְאוּ אֶת הַדָּם וַתִּירְאוּ. ______________

____

____

b. עָמַדְתָּ עַל הָאֶבֶן בְּתוֹךְ הַיָּם. ______________

____

תַּעֲמֹד בֵּין הָעֵצִים הָאֵלֶּה מִבֹּקֶר עַד עֶרֶב. ______________

____

____

תַּעַמְדוּ עִם מִשְׁפְּחוֹתֵיכֶם עַל הַר הַקֹּדֶשׁ. ______________

____

____

אֶעֱמֹד עִם אָחִי אֲשֶׁר בַּמִּדְבָּר וְלֹא אֵלֵךְ. ______________

____

____

c. וַיֹּאמֶר הַכֹּהֵן אֶל הָעֵדָה לֵאמֹר: אַל תַּעַמְדוּ אַחַר הָאֵשׁ הַקְּדוֹשָׁה. ______________

____

וַיֹּאמֶר הָאָב אֶל זַרְעוֹ: אַל תַּעֲלֶה עַל הַדֶּרֶךְ הַזֹּאת. ______________

____

____

וַתֹּאמֶר הָאֵם אֶל בְּנָהּ: תִּזְכֹּר אֶת הַדְּבָרִים אֲשֶׁר אָמַרְתִּי. ______

וַתְּדַבֵּר לֵאָה עִם הַחוֹלִים לֵאמֹר: הָרְפוּאָה תָּבוֹא. הַלְלוּיָהּ!

d. וְשָׁמַעְתָּ אֶת קוֹל הַשּׁוֹפָר וְיָדַעְתָּ כִּי אָנֹכִי מַלְאַךְ הָאֵל. ______

וּשְׁמַעְתֶּם אֶת קוֹלִי וִידַעְתֶּם כִּי יֵשׁ אֱלֹהִים בָּעוֹלָם. ______

וַתִּשְׁמַע אֶת קוֹל הַגֵּר אֲשֶׁר בְּעִירֵךְ וַתִּתֵּן לוֹ לֶחֶם. ______

וַתֶּאֱהָבוּ אֶת הַגֵּר כְּבֵן מִשְׁפַּחְתְּכֶם וַיֵּשֶׁב בְּתוֹכְכֶם בְּשָׁלוֹם.

e. וַתַּעַבְדוּ עִם נַעֲרֵיכֶם וַתּוֹצִיאוּ לֶחֶם מִן הָאָרֶץ. ______

וַעֲבַדְתֶּם כְּגִבּוֹרִים וּבְנִיתֶם אֶת עִירְכֶם הַגְּדוֹלָה. ______

וַאֲהַבְתֶּם אֶת נְשֵׁיכֶם כָּל חַיֵּיכֶם בְּכָל לִבְּכֶם. ____________

____

____

וְאָהַבְתִּי אֶת אֲדוֹנִי בְּכָל לְבָבִי וּבְכָל נַפְשִׁי. ____________

____

____

Translations

a. He lifted/did lift/was lifting/has lifted/had lifted his eyes and then he saw/did see/was seeing/has seen/had seen the blood upon the face of his friend/companion/neighbor/fellow.

You lifted/did lift/were lifting/have lifted/had lifted your eyes and then you saw/did see/were seeing/have seen/had seen the blood of your neighbor.

He lifted/did lift/was lifting his eyes and he saw/did see/was seeing and behold/here [was] blood on his hands.

You lifted/did lift/were lifting your eyes and you saw/did see/were seeing the blood and you feared/did fear/were afraid.

b. You stood/did stand/were standing on the stone in the midst of the sea.

You will/shall/may stand {May you stand} among these trees from morning until evening.

You will/shall/may stand {May you stand} with your families on the mountain of holiness {the holy mountain}.

I will/shall/may {Let me/May I} stand with my brothers who are in the desert/wilderness and I will/shall/may {let me/may I} not go.

c. The priest said/did say/was saying to the congregation/assembly/community saying: Do not stand behind the holy fire.

The father said/did say/was saying to his offspring: Do not ascend/go up on this way/road/path.

The mother said/did say/was saying to her son: You will/shall remember {May you remember} the words that I said/did say/was saying/have said/had said.

Leah spoke/did speak with the sick [ones] saying: The healing will/shall/may come. {May the healing come/Let the healing come.} Hallelujah/Praise Yah!

d. You will/shall/may {May you} hear the sound of the shofar and you will/shall/may know {may you know} that I am the messenger/angel of God.

You will/shall/may {May you} hear my voice and you will/shall/may {may you} know that there is [a] God in the world/universe.

You heard/did hear/were hearing the voice of the stranger/sojourner who is in your city and you gave/did give/were giving to him bread.

You loved/did love the stranger/sojourner like/as a son {member} of your family and he dwelt/did dwell in your midst in peace.

e. You worked/did work/were working with your lads/youths/young men and you brought out bread from the earth.

You will/shall/may {May you} work like mighty ones and you will/shall/may {may you} build your great city.

You will/shall/may {May you} love your wives all your lives with all your heart.

I will/shall/may {May I/Let me} love my lord with all my heart and with all my soul.

FROM OUR TEXTS

"Instead of a Love Poem"

This poem by the modern Hebrew poet Yehuda Amichai takes a biblical verse as its point of departure. "You shall not boil a kid in its mother's milk" is repeated three times in the Torah: in Exodus 23:19, in Exodus 34:26, and in Deuteronomy 14:21. From this threefold repetition were derived the elaborate dietary laws pertaining to the separation of milk and meat. The word תְּבַשֵּׁל is an imperfect "you" form. The word הָיִית in the last line is a feminine perfect "you" form of the root ה־י־ה.

Instead of a Love Poem

FOR CHANA

Just as from "you shall not boil a
kid in its mother's milk,"
they made all the many laws of
kashrut,
but the kid is forgotten and the milk is
forgotten and the mother is forgotten,

so from "I love you"
we made all our life together.
But I have not forgotten you
as you were then.

בִּמְקוֹם שִׁיר אַהֲבָה

לְחַנָּה

כְּמוֹ שֶׁמִּ״לֹא תְבַשֵּׁל גְּדִי בַּחֲלֵב
אִמּוֹ,״
עָשׂוּ אֶת כָּל הַחֻקִּים הָרַבִּים שֶׁל
כַּשְׁרוּת,
אֲבָל הַגְּדִי שָׁכוּחַ וְהֶחָלָב שָׁכוּחַ
וְהָאֵם שְׁכוּחָה,

כָּךְ מֵ״אֲנִי אוֹהֵב אוֹתָךְ״
עָשִׂינוּ אֶת כָּל חַיֵּינוּ יַחְדָּו.
אֲבָל אֲנִי לֹא שָׁכַחְתִּי אוֹתָךְ
כְּפִי שֶׁהָיִית אָז.

Torah Study Text: Deuteronomy 5:6–7, 12–18

The Ten Commandments appear twice in the Torah: in Exodus 20 and in Deuteronomy 5. The second time, they are quoted in a speech by Moses. The wording of the two versions is very close, but there are some differences, especially in the Fourth Commandment regarding the Sabbath.

Verses 8–11, containing part of the Second and the Third Commandments, have been omitted below, in order to shorten our selection.

Read the Hebrew below to see how many of the words you can recognize. This passage does contain words, Hebrew roots, and grammatical concepts that have not yet been introduced. Underline or circle the words, roots, endings, and prefixes that you know.

Deuteronomy 5:6–7

6 אָנֹכִי יְהוָה אֱלֹהֶיךָ אֲשֶׁר הוֹצֵאתִיךָ מֵאֶרֶץ מִצְרַיִם מִבֵּית עֲבָדִים:
7 לֹא יִהְיֶה־לְךָ אֱלֹהִים אֲחֵרִים עַל־פָּנָי:

Deuteronomy 5:12–18

12 שָׁמוֹר אֶת־יוֹם הַשַּׁבָּת לְקַדְּשׁוֹ כַּאֲשֶׁר צִוְּךָ יְהוָה אֱלֹהֶיךָ: 13 שֵׁשֶׁת
יָמִים תַּעֲבֹד וְעָשִׂיתָ כָּל־מְלַאכְתֶּךָ: 14 וְיוֹם הַשְּׁבִיעִי שַׁבָּת לַיהוָה
אֱלֹהֶיךָ לֹא־תַעֲשֶׂה כָל־מְלָאכָה אַתָּה וּבִנְךָ־וּבִתֶּךָ וְעַבְדְּךָ־וַאֲמָתֶךָ
וְשׁוֹרְךָ וַחֲמֹרְךָ וְכָל־בְּהֶמְתֶּךָ וְגֵרְךָ אֲשֶׁר בִּשְׁעָרֶיךָ לְמַעַן יָנוּחַ
עַבְדְּךָ וַאֲמָתְךָ כָּמוֹךָ: 15 וְזָכַרְתָּ כִּי עֶבֶד הָיִיתָ בְּאֶרֶץ מִצְרַיִם וַיֹּצִאֲךָ
יְהוָה אֱלֹהֶיךָ מִשָּׁם בְּיָד חֲזָקָה וּבִזְרֹעַ נְטוּיָה עַל־כֵּן צִוְּךָ יְהוָה
אֱלֹהֶיךָ לַעֲשׂוֹת אֶת־יוֹם הַשַּׁבָּת: 16 כַּבֵּד אֶת־אָבִיךָ וְאֶת־אִמֶּךָ
כַּאֲשֶׁר צִוְּךָ יְהוָה אֱלֹהֶיךָ לְמַעַן יַאֲרִיכֻן יָמֶיךָ וּלְמַעַן יִיטַב לָךְ
עַל הָאֲדָמָה אֲשֶׁר־יְהוָה אֱלֹהֶיךָ נֹתֵן לָךְ: 17 לֹא תִרְצָח וְלֹא תִנְאָף

וְלֹא תִגְנֹב וְלֹא־תַעֲנֶה בְרֵעֲךָ עֵד שָׁוְא׃ [18] וְלֹא תַחְמֹד אֵשֶׁת רֵעֶךָ
וְלֹא תִתְאַוֶּה בֵּית רֵעֶךָ שָׂדֵהוּ וְעַבְדּוֹ וַאֲמָתוֹ שׁוֹרוֹ וַחֲמֹרוֹ
וְכֹל אֲשֶׁר לְרֵעֶךָ׃

Translating the Torah Study Text

Following is our Torah Study Text, Deuteronomy 5:6–7, 12–18, reprinted with a literal translation underneath each word. Using your knowledge of the building blocks of the Hebrew language and the meanings of the words provided below, translate this passage into clear English sentences. Write your translation on the lines following the text. This selection includes some grammatical forms and vocabulary that have not yet been introduced. You will need to rely, in part, on the translations provided.

Deuteronomy 5:6–7

אָנֹכִי	יְהוָה	אֱלֹהֶיךָ	אֲשֶׁר	הוֹצֵאתִיךָ	מֵאֶרֶץ	מִצְרַיִם	מִבֵּית
I	*the Eternal*	*your God*	*who*	*brought you out*	*from land*	*Egypt*	*from house of*

עֲבָדִים׃	לֹא	יִהְיֶה־	לְךָ	אֱלֹהִים	אֲחֵרִים	עַל־	פָּנָי׃
slaves/ servants	*not*	*will be*	*to you*	*God/gods*	*other*	*over*	*my face [me]*

Deuteronomy 5:12–18

שָׁמוֹר	אֶת־יוֹם	הַשַּׁבָּת	לְקַדְּשׁוֹ	כַּאֲשֶׁר
guard/ keep	*day*	*the Sabbath*	*to sanctify it*	*as*

צִוְּךָ	יְהוָה	אֱלֹהֶיךָ׃	שֵׁשֶׁת	יָמִים	תַּעֲבֹד	וְעָשִׂיתָ
has commanded you	*the Eternal*	*your God*	*six*	*days*	*you shall work*	*and you shall do*

כָּל־	מְלַאכְתֶּךָ׃	וְיוֹם	הַשְּׁבִיעִי	שַׁבָּת	לַיהוָה	אֱלֹהֶיךָ	לֹא־
all	*your work*	*and day*	*the seventh*	*Sabbath*	*to/for the Eternal*	*your God*	*not*

תַעֲשֶׂה	כָל־	מְלָאכָה	אַתָּה	וּבִנְךָ־	וּבִתֶּךָ	וְעַבְדְּךָ־
you shall do	*all*	*work*	*you*	*and your son*	*and your daughter*	*and your servant*

וַאֲמָתֶךָ	וְשׁוֹרְךָ	וַחֲמֹרְךָ	וְכָל־	בְּהֶמְתֶּךָ	וְגֵרְךָ
and your maid	*and your ox*	*and your donkey*	*and all*	*your animal/ cattle*	*and your stranger*

אֲשֶׁר	בִּשְׁעָרֶיךָ	לְמַעַן	יָנוּחַ	עַבְדְּךָ	וַאֲמָתְךָ	כָּמוֹךָ׃
who	*in your gates*	*so that*	*may rest*	*your servant*	*and your maid*	*like you*

וְזָכַרְתָּ	כִּי	עֶבֶד	הָיִיתָ	בְּאֶרֶץ	מִצְרַיִם	וַיֹּצִאֲךָ	יְהוָה
and remember	*that*	*slave*	*you were*	*in land*	*Egypt*	*and brought you out*	*the Eternal*

אֱלֹהֶיךָ	מִשָּׁם	בְּיָד	חֲזָקָה	וּבִזְרֹעַ	נְטוּיָה	עַל־כֵּן
your God	*from there*	*with hand*	*strong*	*and with arm*	*outstretched*	*therefore*

צִוְּךָ	יְהוָה	אֱלֹהֶיךָ	לַעֲשׂוֹת	אֶת־יוֹם	הַשַּׁבָּת׃	כַּבֵּד
commanded you	*the Eternal*	*your God*	*to make/ do*	*day*	*the Sabbath*	*honor*

אֶת־אָבִיךָ	וְאֶת־	אִמֶּךָ	כַּאֲשֶׁר	צִוְּךָ	יְהוָה	אֱלֹהֶיךָ	לְמַעַן
your father	*and*	*your mother*	*as*	*commanded you*	*the Eternal*	*your God*	*so that*

יַאֲרִיכֻן	יָמֶיךָ	וּלְמַעַן	יִיטַב	לָךְ	עַל	הָאֲדָמָה	אֲשֶׁר־
be prolonged	*your days*	*and so that*	*it may be well*	*for you*	*on*	*the land*	*that*

יְהוָה	אֱלֹהֶיךָ	נֹתֵן	לָךְ׃	לֹא	תִרְצָח	וְלֹא	תִנְאָף
the Eternal	*your God*	*gives*	*to you*	*not*	*you shall murder*	*and not*	*you shall commit adultery*

וְלֹא	תִגְנֹב	וְלֹא־	תַעֲנֶה	בְרֵעֲךָ	עֵד	שָׁוְא׃	וְלֹא
and not	*you shall steal*	*and not*	*you shall testify*	*against your neighbor/fellow*	*witness*	*vain/ false*	*and not*

תַחְמֹד	אֵשֶׁת	רֵעֶךָ	וְלֹא	תִתְאַוֶּה	בֵּית	רֵעֶךָ
you shall covet/desire	*wife of*	*your neighbor/ fellow*	*and not*	*desire/ crave*	*house of*	*your neighbor/ fellow*

שָׂדֵהוּ	וְעַבְדּוֹ	וַאֲמָתוֹ	שׁוֹרוֹ	וַחֲמֹרוֹ	וְכֹל	אֲשֶׁר
his field	*and his servant*	*and his maid*	*his ox*	*and his donkey*	*and all*	*that*

לְרֵעֶךָ׃
to your neighbor/fellow

TORAH Translations

Compare your translation of Deuteronomy 5:6–7, 12–18 with the Torah translations below.

6 I the Lord *am your God who brought you out of the land of Egypt, the*
house of bondage: 7You shall have no other gods beside Me....

12Observe the sabbath day and keep it holy, as the Lord *your God has commanded*
you. 13Six days you shall labor and do all your work, 14but the seventh day is a sabbath
of the Lord *your God; you shall not do any work—you, your son or your daughter,*
your male or female slave, your ox or your ass, or any of your cattle, or the stranger in
your settlements, so that your male and female slave may rest as you do. 15Remember
that you were a slave in the land of Egypt and the Lord *your God freed you from there*
with a mighty hand and an outstretched arm; therefore the Lord *your God has com-*
manded you to observe the sabbath day.

16Honor your father and your mother, as the Lord *your God has commanded you,*
that you may long endure, and that you may fare well, in the land that the Lord *your*
God is assigning to you.

17You shall not murder.

You shall not commit adultery.

You shall not steal.

You shall not bear false witness against your neighbor.

18You shall not covet your neighbor's wife. You shall not crave your neighbor's house,
or his field, or his male or female slave, or his ox, or his ass, or anything that is your
neighbor's.

JPS Hebrew-English Tanakh: The Traditional Hebrew Text and the New JPS Translation—2d Ed. Philadelphia: Jewish Publication Society, 1999.

6I am Hashem, *your God, Who has taken you out of the land of Egypt, from the house*
of slavery.

7You shall not recognize the gods of others in My Presence....

12Safeguard the Sabbath day to sanctify it, as Hashem, *your God, has commanded*
you. 13Six days shall you labor and accomplish all your work; 14but the seventh day is
Sabbath to Hashem, *your God; you shall not do any work—you, your son, your daugh-*
ter, your slave, your maidservant, your ox, your donkey, and your every animal, and
your convert within your gates, in order that your slave and your maidservant may rest
like you. 15And you shall remember that you were a slave in the land of Egypt, and
Hashem, *your God, has taken you out from there with a strong hand and an out-*

stretched arm; therefore HASHEM, your God, has commanded you to make the Sabbath day.

[16]*Honor your father and your mother, as HASHEM, your God, commanded you, so that your days will be lengthened and so that it will be good for you, upon the land that HASHEM, your God, gives you.*

[17]*You shall not kill; and you shall not commit adultery; and you shall not steal; and you shall not bear vain witness against your fellow.*

[18]*And you shall not covet your fellow's wife, you shall not desire your fellow's house, his field, his slave, his maidservant, his ox, his donkey, or anything that belongs to your fellow.*

THE CHUMASH, ARTSCROLL SERIES, STONE EDITION. BROOKLYN: MESORAH PUBLICATIONS, 1993.

[6]*I am YHWH your God*
who brought you out of the land of Egypt, out of a house of serfs.
[7]*You are not to have other gods beside my presence....*

[12]*Keep the day of Sabbath, by hallowing it,*
as YHWH your God has commanded you.
[13]*For six days you are to serve and to do all your work;*
[14]*but the seventh day*
(is) Sabbath for YHWH your God—
you are not to do any work:
(not) you, nor your son, nor your daughter,
nor your servant, nor your maid,
nor your ox, nor your donkey, nor any of your animals,
nor your sojourner that is in your gates—
in order that your servant and your maid may rest as one-like-yourself.
[15]*You are to bear-in-mind that serf were you in the land of Egypt,*
but YHWH your God took you out from there with a strong hand and with an outstretched arm;
therefore YHWH your God commands you to observe the day of Sabbath.

[16]*Honor your father and your mother,*
as YHWH your God has commanded you,
in order that your days may be prolonged,
and in order that it may go-well with you on the soil that YHWH your God is giving you.
[17]*You are not to murder!*

And you are not to adulter!
And you are not to steal!
And you are not to testify against your neighbor as a lying witness!
[18]*And you are not to desire the wife of your neighbor;*
you are not to crave the house of your neighbor,
his field, or his servant, or his maid, his ox or his donkey,
or anything that belongs to your neighbor!

The Five Books of Moses: A New Translation with Introductions, Commentary, and Notes by Everett Fox. New York: Schocken Books, 1995.

I am the Lord thy God, who brought thee out of the land of Mizrayim, from the house of bondage. Thou shalt have no other gods beside me....

Keep the sabbath day to sanctify it, as the Lord thy God has commanded thee. Six days thou shalt labour, and do all thy work: but the seventh day is the sabbath of the Lord thy God: on it thou shalt not do any work, thou, nor thy son, nor thy daughter, nor thy manservant, nor thy maidservant, nor thy ox, nor thy ass, nor any of thy cattle, nor thy stranger that is within thy gates: that thy manservant and thy maidservant may rest as well as thou. And remember that thou wast a servant in the land of Mizrayim, and that the Lord thy God brought thee out from there with a mighty hand and a stretched out arm: therefore the Lord thy God commanded thee to keep the sabbath day. Honour thy father and thy mother, as the Lord thy God has commanded thee; that thy days may be prolonged, and that it may go well with thee, in the land which the Lord thy God gives thee. Thou shalt not murder. Neither shalt thou commit adultery. Neither shalt thou steal. Neither shalt thou bear false witness against thy neighbour. Neither shalt thou covet thy neighbor's wife, neither shalt thou desire thy neighbour's house, his field, or his manservant, or his maidservant, his ox, or his ass, or anything that is thy neighbour's.

The Jerusalem Bible, published for the Nahum Zeev Williams Family Foundation at Hechal Shlomo, Jerusalem. Jerusalem: Koren Publishers Jerusalem Ltd., 1969.

Vocabulary

Locate each of the following words in the Torah Study Text: Deuteronomy 5:6–7, 12–18.

other, another, different	—	אַחֵר
as, according, when	—	כַּאֲשֶׁר
work, labor, occupation *f*	—	מְלָאכָה

daughter *f* — בַּת

gate *m* — שַׁעַר

in order to, so that, for the sake of — לְמַעַן

Note on the Vocabulary

As with other adjectives, the word אַחֵר has four forms:

אַחֲרוֹת *f pl*   אֲחֵרִים *m pl*   אַחֶרֶת *f sg*   אַחֵר *m sg*

The basic meaning of the root כ־ב־ד is "be heavy," "be weighty," or "be honored." It appears most often in the פִּעֵל pattern with the meaning "honor" or "respect." The participle, perfect, and imperfect forms are all listed in the verb charts in the back of the book.

This root appears in a פִּעֵל command form in the Fifth Commandment:

(verse 16)

honor your father and your mother — כַּבֵּד אֶת־אָבִיךָ וְאֶת־אִמֶּךָ

The following words, both ancient and modern, are derived from the root כ־ב־ד.

heavy — כָּבֵד

liver *(the organ)* — כָּבֵד

heaviness, weight, seriousness, gravity — כֹּבֶד

honor, respect, glory — כָּבוֹד

in honor of — לְכָבוֹד

abundance, riches, precious things, belongings — כְּבוּדָּה

heaviness, weight; slowness, difficulty — כְּבֵדוּת

honoring, respect — כִּבּוּד

honored, honorable, respected — מְכֻבָּד

The root נ־ו־ח appears in the פָּעַל pattern with the basic meaning "rest." In the הִפְעִיל pattern, it means "cause to rest," "pacify," or "calm." The participle, perfect, and imperfect forms of the root נ־ו־ח in both the פָּעַל and הִפְעִיל patterns can be found in the verb charts in the back of the book. This root appears once in our Torah Study Text, in the Fourth Commandment, at the end of verse 14:

so that your servant and your maid may rest like you	—	לְמַעַן יָנוּחַ עַבְדְּךָ וַאֲמָתְךָ כָּמוֹךָ

The following words and expressions, both ancient and modern, are derived from the root נ־ו־ח. The middle root letter ו drops out or appears as the vowel וֹ or וּ in many words formed from this root.

quietness, rest, contentment	—	נַחַת
satisfaction, pleasure (Yiddish: *nachas*)	—	נַחַת רוּחַ
comfortable, congenial, pleasant	—	נוֹחַ
Noah	—	נֹחַ
restful, quiescent	—	נָח
rest, calm	—	נוּחָה
convenience, comfort	—	נוֹחוּת
aroma, pleasant scent	—	רֵיחַ נִיחוֹחַ
repose, relief; reduction of price, discount	—	הֲנָחָה
resting place, rest, sanctuary, repose	—	מָנוֹחַ
Manoach *(biblical name, the father of Samson)*	—	מָנוֹחַ
resting place, rest, quiet, calm, tranquility	—	מְנוּחָה
Good night! (a night of rest)	—	לֵיל מְנוּחָה
still waters	—	מֵי מְנוּחוֹת

TORAH Commentary

The words עַל פָּנָי at the end of verse 7 are difficult to understand. Literally, they mean "over/on/about my face." Various translations render them "beside Me," "before me," "beside my presence," and "in My presence." Rashi offers another explanation.

עַל פָּנָי—*in every place where I am, and that is the whole universe. Another explanation: as long as I exist.*

RASHI ON DEUTERONOMY 5:7

Verse 15 links our remembrance of slavery in Egypt with God's commandment לַעֲשׂוֹת, "to make," the Sabbath.

Several times the Torah refers to Shabbos with the word "לַעֲשׂוֹת, to make (the Shabbos)," as though there were something active about Shabbos, although it would seem that the salient feature of Shabbos is complete rest or lack of activity.

...The Midrash states that while Moses was still in the good graces of Pharoah, he convinced the Egyptian king to grant the Israelite slaves a day of rest. He argued that slaves who are overworked and exhausted cannot be productive. The day of rest would actually enable them to turn out a better quantity and quality of work. Moses then selected the seventh day of the week as the day of rest, and the Israelites observed it as "the day of Moses" (Shemos Rabbah 1:32).

The idea of a day of rest is essentially a secular concept. One rests so that one may recharge one's batteries in order to increase one's work efficiency for the following week. The day of rest therefore is a means rather than an end. Rest is thus subservient to work.

The Torah concept of Shabbos is just the reverse. One works six days in order to be able to have a Shabbos.

...Shabbos is a day of spiritual growth and development. It is a day when, through prayer and study of Torah, one should be able to create a new self, a person more refined than one had been heretofore. Shabbos is passive only in the sense of abstinence from work, but that abstinence is not sufficient. It must be used to enable one to make oneself into something finer and more spiritual. This is what the Torah means by repeatedly using the expression "to make" the Shabbos....

...[B]ecause one might observe the Shabbos only with abstinence from work, resting in order to renew one's strength in preparation for the work week, the Torah goes on to say, "Remember how it was in Egypt when you were slaves" (when the passive Shabbos, the 'day of Moses,' was adequate simply as a day of rest). But now that G-d has delivered you from slavery, He is therefore telling you, "to make." Make *the Shabbos an active day of spiritual achievement and creation.*

RABBI ABRAHAM J. TWERSKI, M.D., *LIVING EACH WEEK*. BROOKLYN: MESORAH PUBLICATIONS LTD., 1992.

The commandment לֹא תִרְצָח, "you shall not murder," is a general statement, without qualifying or limiting conditions.

> *I heard from a great Torah scholar that the reason the Torah stated "You shall not kill" without specifying that one is not permitted to kill by means of a stone or a sword, etc., is to teach us that one is not even permitted to kill another person by persecuting or humiliating him.*
>
> *Torah Gems*, comp. Aharon Yaakov Greenberg, trans. by R. Dr. Shmuel Himelstein. Tel Aviv and Brooklyn: Yavneh Publishing House, Chemed Books, 1998.

> *Every person understands the Torah at his or her own level. There were those standing at Mount Sinai who heard the commandment* לֹא תִרְצָח *and understood it simply as "thou shalt not murder." And there were those at a slightly higher level who heard* לֹא תִרְצָח *and understood it to mean "you should not embarass anyone in public." And there were those at a still higher level who heard* לֹא תִרְצַח *and understood it to mean "you should not lose your temper at anyone." And those at the highest level heard* לֹא תִרְצָח *and understood that it meant "you should not ignore another person."*
>
> Chasidic teaching related to the author by Rabbi Sholom Brodt, who received it from Rabbi Shlomo Carlebach.

Exercises

1. Make flash cards for each of the new vocabulary words and Hebrew roots introduced in this chapter, or use the flash card set published as a companion to this book. Review the cards to learn all of them.

2. Draw a line connecting each Hebrew word to its English translation. For some words, there can be more than one correct translation.

another	כַּאֲשֶׁר
gate	שַׁעַר
for the sake of	לְמַעַן
when	מְלָאכָה
daughter	בַּת
in order to	אַחֵר
as	
work	
different	
labor	

3. On the left are plural forms of words introduced as vocabulary in this chapter. Draw a line connecting each plural word to its singular form. Translate both into English.

________________	בָּנוֹת	מְלָאכָה	________________
________________	אֲחֵרִים	שַׁעַר	________________
________________	שְׁעָרִים	בַּת	________________
________________	מְלָאכוֹת	אַחֵר	________________

4. Read and translate the following groups of words.

________________	b. שַׁעַר הַשָּׁמַיִם	________________	a. בַּת צִיּוֹן
________________	שַׁעֲרֵי יְרוּשָׁלַיִם	________________	בְּנוֹת כְּנַעַן
________________	שַׁעֲרֵי צֶדֶק	________________	בְּנוֹתֵיהֶם
________________	שְׁעָרֶיךָ	________________	בִּתִּי
________________	שַׁעֲרֵיכֶם	________________	בִּתֵּנוּ

c. לְמַעַן שְׁמוֹ ______________
לְמַעַן אַחַי וְרֵעָי ______________
____
לְמַעַן תִּזְכְּרוּ ______________
לְמַעַן חַיֶּיךָ ______________
לְמַעַן בְּרִיתוֹ ______________

d. מְלַאכְתּוֹ ______________
מִכָּל מְלַאכְתּוֹ ______________
____
מְלַאכְתֶּךָ ______________
מְלֶאכֶת עוֹלָמִים ______________
____
מְלֶאכֶת רֵעֵהוּ ______________

e. זֶרַע אַחֵר ______________
לֵב אַחֵר ______________
רוּחַ אַחֶרֶת ______________
____
שָׁנָה אַחֶרֶת ______________
____
יָמִים אֲחֵרִים ______________
____

f. כַּאֲשֶׁר דִּבַּרְתִּי ______________
כַּאֲשֶׁר צִוָּה הָאָדוֹן ______________
____
כַּאֲשֶׁר שְׁמַעְתֶּם ______________
____
כַּאֲשֶׁר עָשָׂה ______________
כַּאֲשֶׁר תִּרְאֶה ______________

5. Identify the root of each of the following verbs and whether it is a perfect, imperfect, or participle form. Translate.

Translation	Form	Root	Verb
			בָּאִים
			נָחִים
			מְנִיחִים
			מְכַבְּדִים
			יָנוּחַ
			תָּנוּחוּ
			תְּכַבְּדוּ

______________	______________	______________	אֲכַבֵּד
______________	______________	______________	נָשָׂאתָ
______________	______________	______________	נַחְתָּ
______________	______________	______________	נַחְתֶּם
______________	______________	______________	הֵנַחְתָּ

EXTRA CREDIT

The Fourth Commandment

As mentioned earlier, there are two different versions of the Ten Commandments in the Torah, in Exodus 20 and in Deuteronomy 5. The two versions differ only slightly in wording, with the exception of the Fourth Commandment, the commandment regarding the Sabbath. In Exodus 20:11, the rationale provided for the observance of the Sabbath is that God created the world in six days and then rested on the seventh. In Deuteronomy 5:15, Sabbath observance is linked to the memory of redemption from slavery in Egypt, and the phrase לְמַעַן יָנוּחַ עַבְדְּךָ וַאֲמָתְךָ כָּמוֹךָ, "so that your servant and your maid may rest like you," appears in Deuteronomy 5:14, where it is absent in the parallel verse in Exodus 20:10. Even the initial wording of the Fourth Commandment differs: in Exodus 20:8, we are told זָכוֹר, "remember," the Sabbath day, whereas in Deuteronomy 5:12, we are told שָׁמוֹר, "guard/keep," the Sabbath day.

According to the Midrash (*Mechilta, Bachodesh* 7), both שָׁמוֹר, "guard/keep," and זָכוֹר, "remember," were uttered simultaneously as one word by God and were heard simultaneously by the Children of Israel at the giving of the Ten Commandments at Mount Sinai. This midrash underlies the first verse of the Sabbath hymn L'cha Dodi, which states:

שָׁמוֹר וְזָכוֹר בְּדִבּוּר אֶחָד, הִשְׁמִיעָנוּ אֵל הַמְיֻחָד

"'guard/keep' and 'remember' in one utterance, the singular God caused us to hear."

The two differing rationales for Sabbath observance are also reflected in the Shabbat evening קִדּוּשׁ, "sanctification," the blessing said over a cup of wine or grape juice to sanctify the Sabbath. In this blessing, the Sabbath day is described as both זִכָּרוֹן לְמַעֲשֵׂה בְרֵאשִׁית, "a remembrance of the act of Creation," and זֵכֶר לִיצִיאַת מִצְרָיִם, "a reminder of the Exodus from Egypt."

Torah Study Text: Vocabulary and Root Review

This unit's Torah Study Text, Deuteronomy 5:6–7, 12–18, is reprinted below, highlighting the new vocabulary words as well as the words formed from the new Hebrew roots introduced in Chapter 7. Read this passage again, recalling the meaning of each of the highlighted words or roots.

Deuteronomy 5:6–7

6 אָנֹכִי יְהוָה אֱלֹהֶיךָ אֲשֶׁר הוֹצֵאתִיךָ מֵאֶרֶץ מִצְרַיִם מִבֵּית עֲבָדִים׃
7 לֹא יִהְיֶה־לְךָ אֱלֹהִים **אֲחֵרִים** עַל־פָּנָי׃

Deuteronomy 5:12–18

12 שָׁמוֹר אֶת־יוֹם הַשַּׁבָּת לְקַדְּשׁוֹ **כַּאֲשֶׁר** צִוְּךָ יְהוָה אֱלֹהֶיךָ׃ 13 שֵׁשֶׁת
יָמִים תַּעֲבֹד וְעָשִׂיתָ כָּל־**מְלַאכְתֶּךָ**׃ 14 וְיוֹם הַשְּׁבִיעִי שַׁבָּת לַיהוָה
אֱלֹהֶיךָ לֹא־תַעֲשֶׂה כָל־**מְלָאכָה** אַתָּה וּבִנְךָ־**וּבִתֶּךָ** וְעַבְדְּךָ־וַאֲמָתֶךָ
וְשׁוֹרְךָ וַחֲמֹרְךָ וְכָל־בְּהֶמְתֶּךָ וְגֵרְךָ אֲשֶׁר **בִּשְׁעָרֶיךָ** **לְמַעַן יָנוּחַ**
עַבְדְּךָ וַאֲמָתְךָ כָּמוֹךָ׃ 15 וְזָכַרְתָּ כִּי עֶבֶד הָיִיתָ בְּאֶרֶץ מִצְרַיִם וַיֹּצִאֲךָ
יְהוָה אֱלֹהֶיךָ מִשָּׁם בְּיָד חֲזָקָה וּבִזְרֹעַ נְטוּיָה עַל־כֵּן צִוְּךָ יְהוָה
אֱלֹהֶיךָ לַעֲשׂוֹת אֶת־יוֹם הַשַּׁבָּת׃ 16 **כַּבֵּד** אֶת־אָבִיךָ וְאֶת־אִמֶּךָ
כַּאֲשֶׁר צִוְּךָ יְהוָה אֱלֹהֶיךָ **לְמַעַן** יַאֲרִיכֻן יָמֶיךָ **וּלְמַעַן** יִיטַב לָךְ
עַל הָאֲדָמָה אֲשֶׁר־יְהוָה אֱלֹהֶיךָ נֹתֵן לָךְ׃ 17 לֹא תִרְצָח וְלֹא תִנְאָף
וְלֹא תִגְנֹב וְלֹא־תַעֲנֶה בְרֵעֲךָ עֵד שָׁוְא׃ 18 וְלֹא תַחְמֹד אֵשֶׁת רֵעֶךָ
וְלֹא תִתְאַוֶּה בֵּית רֵעֶךָ שָׂדֵהוּ וְעַבְדּוֹ וַאֲמָתוֹ שׁוֹרוֹ וַחֲמֹרוֹ
וְכֹל אֲשֶׁר לְרֵעֶךָ׃

Building Blocks

"Have" and "Not Have" in Hebrew

There is no verb "to have" in Hebrew. Instead of using a verb, the preposition ל is used:

Sarah has a daughter. (*literally:* To Sarah [is] a daughter.) — לְשָׂרָה בַּת.

I have many brothers. (*literally:* To me [are] many brothers.) — לִי אַחִים רַבִּים.

The word יֵשׁ, "there is/there are," may appear with the preposition ל:

Sarah has a daughter. (*literally:* There is to Sarah a daughter.) — יֵשׁ לְשָׂרָה בַּת.

I have many brothers. (*literally:* There are to me many brothers.) — יֵשׁ לִי אַחִים רַבִּים.

The word אֵין, "there is not/there are not," is used with the preposition ל to express "not have":

Sarah does not have a daughter. (*literally:* There is not to Sarah a daughter.) — אֵין לְשָׂרָה בַּת.

I do not have many brothers. (*literally:* There are not to me many brothers.) — אֵין לִי אַחִים רַבִּים.

"Have" and "Not Have" in the Perfect and Imperfect

In the first examples given above, there is no indication in the Hebrew of any time frame. Although we translated those examples into English in the present tense, they could be translated otherwise, depending upon the context:

Sarah had/has/will have a daughter. (*literally:* To Sarah a daughter.) — לְשָׂרָה בַּת.

I had/have/will have many brothers. (*literally:* To me many brothers.) — לִי אַחִים רַבִּים.

To express "have" in different tenses, perfect or imperfect forms of the verb ה־י־ה may be used with the preposition לְ. The form of the verb ה־י־ה matches whatever is possessed:

Sarah had a daughter. (*literally:* Was to Sarah a daughter.)	—	הָיְתָה לְשָׂרָה בַּת.
Sarah will/shall/may have a son. (*literally:* Will/shall/may be to Sarah a son.)	—	יִהְיֶה לְשָׂרָה בֵּן.
I had many brothers. (*literally:* Were to me many brothers.)	—	הָיוּ לִי אַחִים רַבִּים.
I will/shall/may have many brothers. (*literally:* Will/shall/ may be to me many brothers.)	—	יִהְיוּ לִי אַחִים רַבִּים.

The word לֹא, "not," is used with the perfect or imperfect forms of ה־י־ה to express "not have":

Sarah will/shall/may not have a daughter.	—	לֹא יִהְיֶה לְשָׂרָה בֵּן.
I did not have many brothers.	—	לֹא הָיוּ לִי אַחִים רַבִּים.

אֲשֶׁר

The word אֲשֶׁר, "that/who/which," is also used with the preposition לְ to indicate possession:

all that is his, everything he has (*literally:* all that is to him)	—	כֹּל אֲשֶׁר לוֹ
her father's house, the house that belongs to her father (*literally:* the house that is to her father)	—	הַבַּיִת אֲשֶׁר לְאָבִיהָ

Torah Study Text with Building Blocks

Following are excerpts, Deuteronomy 5:6–7 and 18, from this unit's Torah Study Text, reprinted with the new Building Blocks highlighted. Reread these verses, noting the use of the preposition ל to express possession. A translation is provided below for only the highlighted Building Blocks. Remember that there could be other possible translations. For a full translation of the verses, refer back to Chapter 7.

Deuteronomy 5:6–7

6 אָנֹכִי יְהוָה אֱלֹהֶיךָ אֲשֶׁר הוֹצֵאתִיךָ מֵאֶרֶץ מִצְרַיִם מִבֵּית עֲבָדִים׃

7 **לֹא יִהְיֶה־לְךָ** אֱלֹהִים אֲחֵרִים עַל־פָּנָי׃

Deuteronomy 5:18

18 וְלֹא תַחְמֹד אֵשֶׁת רֵעֶךָ וְלֹא תִתְאַוֶּה בֵּית רֵעֶךָ שָׂדֵהוּ וְעַבְדּוֹ
וַאֲמָתוֹ שׁוֹרוֹ וַחֲמֹרוֹ וְ**כֹל אֲשֶׁר לְרֵעֶךָ**׃

you shall not have (*literally:* shall not be to you)	—	לֹא יִהְיֶה־לְךָ
all that is your neighbor's (*literally:* all that is to your neighbor)	—	כֹּל אֲשֶׁר לְרֵעֶךָ

Additional Reading and Translation Practice

Translate the following excerpts from the Bible and the prayer book, using the extra vocabulary words provided. Check your translations against the English translations that follow.

1. From יוֹם זֶה לְיִשְׂרָאֵל—This traditional Shabbat table hymn is sometimes included in Shabbat services as a concluding song. Following is the chorus, in which the preposition ל attached to the word יִשְׂרָאֵל can be understood as indicating possession.

light (*a variation of the word* אוֹר)	—	אוֹרָה
joy	—	שִׂמְחָה
rest (*from the root* נ־ו־ח)	—	מְנוּחָה

יוֹם זֶה לְיִשְׂרָאֵל אוֹרָה וְשִׂמְחָה, שַׁבַּת מְנוּחָה.

---

2. From אֲדוֹן עוֹלָם—This well-known hymn in praise of God is sung at the conclusion of Shabbat and holiday services. The following excerpt is from the third verse. The phrase וְלוֹ הָעֹז is a possessive phrase.

second	—	שֵׁנִי
to compare	—	לְהַמְשִׁיל
to join together	—	לְהַחְבִּירָה
without	—	בְּלִי
beginning	—	רֵאשִׁית
end	—	תַּכְלִית
power	—	עֹז
dominion	—	מִשְׂרָה

וְהוּא אֶחָד, וְאֵין שֵׁנִי לְהַמְשִׁיל לוֹ, לְהַחְבִּירָה, בְּלִי רֵאשִׁית, בְּלִי
תַכְלִית, וְלוֹ הָעֹז וְהַמִּשְׂרָה.

____

____

3. לְךָ יְיָ (I Chronicles 29:11)—This verse in praise of God is sung during the processional with the Torah scrolls prior to the reading from the Torah. The word לְךָ indicates possession.

greatness	—	גְּדֻלָּה
splendor	—	תִּפְאֶרֶת
triumph	—	נֵצַח
majesty	—	הוֹד
sovereignty	—	מַמְלָכָה
[one who] is exalted (*from the root* נ־שׂ־א, lift)	—	מִתְנַשֵּׂא

לְךָ יְיָ הַגְּדֻלָּה וְהַגְּבוּרָה וְהַתִּפְאֶרֶת וְהַנֵּצַח וְהַהוֹד, כִּי־כֹל בַּשָּׁמַיִם
וּבָאָרֶץ, לְךָ יְיָ הַמַּמְלָכָה וְהַמִּתְנַשֵּׂא לְכֹל לְרֹאשׁ:

____

____

4. From יִגְדַּל—This thirteen-line hymn based on Maimonides' Thirteen Principles of Faith is included as a concluding song on Shabbat and festivals. The following comes from the second and third lines, containing assertions about God and statements of "not have" using the אֵין ל form.

singular	—	יָחִיד
singularity	—	יִחוּד
hidden, concealed, unknown	—	נֶעְלָם
also	—	גַּם
end	—	סוֹף
oneness	—	אַחְדוּת
form	—	דְמוּת
body	—	גּוּף
אֵין לוֹ	=	אֵינוֹ

אֶחָד וְאֵין יָחִיד כְּיִחוּדוֹ, נֶעְלָם וְגַם אֵין סוֹף לְאַחְדוּתוֹ:
אֵין לוֹ דְמוּת הַגּוּף וְאֵינוֹ גּוּף...

____

____

5. From אֱמֶת וְיַצִּיב—This blessing on the theme of redemption comes after the *Shema* in the morning service. The אֵין ל form appears with the meaning "not have."

first	—	רִאשׁוֹן
last	—	אַחֲרוֹן
except for you	—	מִבַּלְעָדֶיךָ
redeemer	—	גּוֹאֵל

אֱמֶת אַתָּה הוּא רִאשׁוֹן וְאַתָּה הוּא אַחֲרוֹן, וּמִבַּלְעָדֶיךָ אֵין לָנוּ
מֶלֶךְ גּוֹאֵל וּמוֹשִׁיעַ...

____

____

6. I Samuel 1:1–2—This passage is the beginning of the Haftarah (the selection from the books of the Prophets) read on the first morning of Rosh HaShanah.

I Samuel 1:1

Ramatayim Tzofim *(a place name)*	—	הָרָמָתַיִם צוֹפִים
Ephraim	—	אֶפְרָיִם
Elkanah *(a personal name)*	—	אֶלְקָנָה
Y'rocham *(a personal name)*	—	יְרֹחָם
Elihu *(a personal name)*	—	אֱלִיהוּא
Tochu *(a personal name)*	—	תֹּחוּ
Tzuf *(a personal name)*	—	צוּף
an Ephraimite (a person from Ephraim)	—	אֶפְרָתִי

וַיְהִי אִישׁ אֶחָד מִן־הָרָמָתַיִם צוֹפִים מֵהַר אֶפְרָיִם, וּשְׁמוֹ אֶלְקָנָה
בֶּן־יְרֹחָם בֶּן־אֱלִיהוּא בֶּן־תֹּחוּ בֶּן־צוּף, אֶפְרָתִי׃

I Samuel 1:2

two	—	שְׁתֵּי
Chanah *(a personal name)*	—	חַנָּה
second	—	שֵׁנִית
P'ninah *(a personal name)*	—	פְּנִנָּה
children	—	יְלָדִים

וְלוֹ שְׁתֵּי נָשִׁים, שֵׁם אַחַת חַנָּה וְשֵׁם הַשֵּׁנִית פְּנִנָּה, וַיְהִי לִפְנִנָּה
יְלָדִים וּלְחַנָּה אֵין יְלָדִים׃

Translations

1. From יוֹם זֶה לְיִשְׂרָאֵל—This day is for Israel {This day is Israel's/Israel has this day} light and joy, a Sabbath of rest.
2. From אֲדוֹן עוֹלָם—And He {God} is One, and there is no second, to compare to Him {God}, to join together, without beginning, without end, and to Him/God are {His/God's are *or* He/God has} the power and the dominion.
3. לְךָ יְיָ (I Chronicles 29:11)—To You, Eternal, are {Yours are/You have} the greatness and the might and the splendor and the triumph and the majesty, that are all in the heavens and on the earth, to You, Eternal, is {Yours is/You have} the sovereignty and [You are] the [One who] is exalted for {over} all for {as} head.
4. From יִגְדַּל—[God is] One and there is none singular like His {God's} singularity, hidden/concealed/unknown and also there is no end to His {God's} oneness {God's oneness has no end}. There is not to Him/God {He/God does not have} a form of the body {bodily form} and there is not to Him/God {He/God does not have} a body...
5. From אֱמֶת וְיַצִּיב—Truth [it is that] You are first and You are last, and except for You there is not to us {we do not have} a sovereign, redeemer, and savior...
6. I Samuel 1:1—[There] was one man from Ramatayim Tzofim from Mount Ephraim and his name was Elkanah son of Y'rocham son of Elihu son of Tochu son of Tzuf, an Ephratite.

   I Samuel 1:2—And to him {he had} two wives, [the] name of one Chanah and the name of the second P'ninah, and there was to P'ninah {P'ninah had} children and to Chanah there are not children {Chanah had no children}.

Exercises

1. In each of the following sentences, circle the one form in the parentheses that is grammatically correct. Translate.

a. (יֵשׁ, הָיוּ, הָיְתָה) לִי בֵּן. ________________

b. לְרָחֵל (הָיָה, הָיְתָה, הָיוּ) אֵם טוֹבָה. ________________

____

c. (הָיָה, הָיוּ, יִהְיֶה) לָנוּ עֵצִים אַחַר שַׁעֲרֵנוּ. ________________

____

d. לָעָם (הָיְתָה, לֹא תִהְיֶה, יֵשׁ) נָבִיא. ________________

e. (יִהְיוּ, לֹא הָיְתָה, לֹא הָיוּ) לְאַבְרָהָם מְזוּזָה בְּבֵיתוֹ. ________________

____

f. (לֹא הָיָה, אֵין, לֹא הָיְתָה) לָכֶם עֲבָדִים רַבִּים. ____________

g. (יֵשׁ, הָיוּ, לֹא יִהְיֶה) רְפוּאָה לַחוֹלִים. ____________

h. (יִהְיֶה, יִהְיוּ, תִּהְיֶה) לְךָ מִשְׁפָּחָה גְּדוֹלָה. ____________

i. (תִּהְיֶה, לֹא יִהְיֶה, הָיוּ) לָנוּ דָּם בְּיָדֵינוּ. ____________

j. (יִהְיוּ, הָיָה, תִּהְיֶה) לָהֶם רַחֲמִים בְּנַפְשׁוֹתֵיהֶם. ____________

2. Read and translate the following groups of sentences. Remember the use of the reversing *vav* prefix. Check your translations against those that follow.

a. אֲנִי מְכַבֵּד אֶת הַגֵּר בְּעִירִי. ____________

אֲנַחְנוּ מְכַבְּדִים אֶת מַלְכֵּנוּ. ____________

מִי גָּדוֹל? הַמְכַבֵּד אֶת כָּל אָדָם. ____________

תְּכַבֵּד אֶת אַדְמָתְךָ הַמּוֹצִיאָה לֶחֶם וּפֵרוֹת. ____________

b. וַיָּנוּחוּ הַמַּלְאָכִים בַּדֶּרֶךְ. ____________

וַיָּנַח הַנַּעַר בָּעֶרֶב. ____________

וַתַּעַשׂ בִּתֵּנוּ אֶת כָּל מְלַאכְתָּהּ וַתָּנַח.

אָנוּחַ בַּלַּיְלָה לְמַעַן אֶעֱבֹד בַּבֹּקֶר.

c. הַאִם הֵנִיחָה אֶת בְּנוֹתֶיהָ כַּאֲשֶׁר דִּבְּרָה.

וְהֵנַחְתָּ אֶת בִּתְּךָ כַּאֲשֶׁר תִּשָּׂא אוֹתָהּ.

אָנֹכִי הֵנַחְתִּי אֶת בָּנַי כַּאֲשֶׁר הֶאֱכַלְתִּי אוֹתָם.

יֵשׁ רוּחַ אַחֶרֶת בְּתוֹךְ הָעֵדָה וְזֹאת מְנִיחָה אֶת הָעָם.

d. לַכֹּהֵן בַּיִת בַּמִּדְבָּר אֲשֶׁר בָּנָה מֵאֶבֶן.

אֵין לַכֹּהֵן שָׁם בַּיִת מֵעֵץ.

הַבַּיִת אֲשֶׁר לַכֹּהֵן לֹא הָיָה כַּבַּיִת אֲשֶׁר לְרֵעֵהוּ.

אַל תִּבְנוּ לָנוּ בַּיִת כָּמוֹהוּ.

e. יֵשׁ לָכֶם אֵשׁ בְּעֵינֵיכֶם וְחֵטְא בִּלְבָבוֹתֵיכֶם.

לֹא הָיוּ לָהֶם אֵשׁ בְּעֵינֵיהֶם וְחֵטְא בִּלְבָבוֹתֵיהֶם.

לֹא יִהְיֶה לִי חֵטְא בְּלִבִּי בַּמָּקוֹם הַקָּדוֹשׁ הַזֶּה. ______________

____

זֹאת אַדְמַת קֹדֶשׁ כִּי יֵשׁ תּוֹרָה וּמִשְׁפָּט בַּמָּקוֹם הַזֶּה. __________

____

Translations

a. I honor/do honor/am honoring {respect/do respect/am respecting} the stranger/sojourner in my city.

We honor/do honor/are honoring {respect/do respect/are respecting} our king.

Who is great? The [one who] honors/respects every human being {all humankind}.

You will/shall/may honor/respect {May you honor/respect} your land/earth that {the one that} brings out bread and fruit.

b. The messengers rested/did rest/were resting in the road {on the way}.

The lad/youth/young man rested/did rest/was resting in the evening.

Our daughter did/was doing/had done all her work/labor and she rested/did rest/was resting.

I will/shall/may rest {May I/Let me rest} in the night {at night} so that I may work in the morning.

c. The mother calmed/did calm/was calming/has calmed/had calmed {pacified/caused to rest} her daughters as/when she spoke/did speak/was speaking/has spoken/had spoken.

You will/shall/may {May you} calm/cause to rest/pacify your daughter as/according as/when you will/shall/may lift/carry her.

I calmed/did calm/was calming/have calmed/had calmed {pacified/caused to rest} my children/sons as/when I fed/did feed/was feeding/have fed/had fed them.

There is another/different spirit/wind in the midst of/within the congregation/assembly/community and this calms/does calm/is calming {pacifying, causing to rest} the people.

d. The priest has {To the priest is} a house in the desert/wilderness that he built/has built/had built from stone.

The priest doesn't have {There is not to the priest} there a house from {of} wood.

The house of the priest {The house that is to the priest} was not like the house of {the house that is to} his neighbor/friend/companion/fellow.

Don't build for us a house like it.

e. You have {There is to you} fire in your eyes and sin in your hearts.

They did not have {There were not to them} fire in their eyes and sin in their hearts.

I will/shall/may {May I/Let me} not have {There will/shall/may not be to me} sin in my heart in this holy place.

This is holy earth/ground/land {This is earth/ground/land of holiness} because/for there are Torah/teaching/law and justice/judgment/law in this place.

This is a poem by Zelda Mishkovsky, a modern Hebrew poet born in 1914, who emigrated from Chernigov, in the Ukraine, to Palestine in 1925. The Hebrew way of expressing possession, using the word יֵשׁ and the preposition לְ, recurs throughout the poem.

Every Man Has a Name	**לְכָל אִישׁ יֵשׁ שֵׁם**
Every man has a name	לְכָל אִישׁ יֵשׁ שֵׁם
that God gave to him	שֶׁנָּתַן לוֹ אֱלֹהִים
and that his father and his mother gave him	וְנָתְנוּ לוֹ אָבִיו וְאִמּוֹ
Every man has a name	לְכָל אִישׁ יֵשׁ שֵׁם
that his stature and his way of smiling have given him	שֶׁנָּתְנוּ לוֹ קוֹמָתוֹ וְאֹפֶן חִיּוּכוֹ
and the cloth has given him	וְנָתַן לוֹ הָאָרִיג
Every man has a name	לְכָל אִישׁ יֵשׁ שֵׁם
that the mountains have given him	שֶׁנָּתְנוּ לוֹ הֶהָרִים
and his walls have given him	וְנָתְנוּ לוֹ כְּתָלָיו
Every man has a name	לְכָל אִישׁ יֵשׁ שֵׁם
that the planets have given him	שֶׁנָּתְנוּ לוֹ הַמַּזָּלוֹת
and his neighbors have given him	וְנָתְנוּ לוֹ שְׁכֵנָיו
Every man has a name	לְכָל אִישׁ יֵשׁ שֵׁם
that his sins have given him	שֶׁנָּתְנוּ לוֹ חֲטָאָיו
and his yearning has given him	וְנָתְנָה לוֹ כְּמִיהָתוֹ
Every man has a name	לְכָל אִישׁ יֵשׁ שֵׁם
that his enemies have given him	שֶׁנָּתְנוּ לוֹ שׂוֹנְאָיו
and his love has given him	וְנָתְנָה לוֹ אַהֲבָתוֹ
Every man has a name	לְכָל אִישׁ יֵשׁ שֵׁם
that his festivals have given him	שֶׁנָּתְנוּ לוֹ חַגָּיו

and his occupation has given him	וְנָתְנָה לוֹ מְלַאכְתּוֹ
Every man has a name	לְכָל אִישׁ יֵשׁ שֵׁם
that the seasons of the year have given him	שֶׁנָּתְנוּ לוֹ תְּקוּפוֹת הַשָּׁנָה
and his blindness has given him	וְנָתַן לוֹ עִוְּרוֹנוֹ
Every man has a name	לְכָל אִישׁ יֵשׁ שֵׁם
that the sea has given him	שֶׁנָּתַן לוֹ הַיָּם
and his death has given him.	וְנָתַן לוֹ מוֹתוֹ.

Torah Study Text: Deuteronomy 30:11–16, 19

Deuteronomy 3:11–16, 19 is part of Moses' final address to the Children of Israel, at the end of their forty years in the wilderness, just prior to his death and their entry into the Promised Land. It includes the famous exhortation *"Choose life!"*, read in Reform synagogues on the morning of Yom Kippur.

Read the Hebrew below to see how many of the words you can recognize. This passage does contain words, Hebrew roots, and grammatical concepts that have not yet been introduced. Underline or circle the words, roots, endings, and prefixes that you know.

Deuteronomy 30:11–16

11 כִּי הַמִּצְוָה הַזֹּאת אֲשֶׁר אָנֹכִי מְצַוְּךָ הַיּוֹם לֹא־נִפְלֵאת הִוא מִמְּךָ
וְלֹא־רְחֹקָה הִוא׃ 12 לֹא בַשָּׁמַיִם הִוא לֵאמֹר מִי יַעֲלֶה־לָּנוּ הַשָּׁמַיְמָה
וְיִקָּחֶהָ לָּנוּ וְיַשְׁמִעֵנוּ אֹתָהּ וְנַעֲשֶׂנָּה׃ 13 וְלֹא־מֵעֵבֶר לַיָּם הִוא לֵאמֹר
מִי יַעֲבָר־לָנוּ אֶל־עֵבֶר הַיָּם וְיִקָּחֶהָ לָּנוּ וְיַשְׁמִעֵנוּ אֹתָהּ וְנַעֲשֶׂנָּה׃
14 כִּי־קָרוֹב אֵלֶיךָ הַדָּבָר מְאֹד בְּפִיךָ וּבִלְבָבְךָ לַעֲשֹׂתוֹ׃ 15 רְאֵה נָתַתִּי
לְפָנֶיךָ הַיּוֹם אֶת־הַחַיִּים וְאֶת־הַטּוֹב וְאֶת־הַמָּוֶת וְאֶת־הָרָע׃ 16 אֲשֶׁר
אָנֹכִי מְצַוְּךָ הַיּוֹם לְאַהֲבָה אֶת־יְהוָה אֱלֹהֶיךָ לָלֶכֶת בִּדְרָכָיו
וְלִשְׁמֹר מִצְוֹתָיו וְחֻקֹּתָיו וּמִשְׁפָּטָיו וְחָיִיתָ וְרָבִיתָ וּבֵרַכְךָ יְהוָה
אֱלֹהֶיךָ בָּאָרֶץ אֲשֶׁר־אַתָּה בָא־שָׁמָּה לְרִשְׁתָּהּ׃

Deuteronomy 30:19

הַעִדֹתִי בָכֶם הַיּוֹם אֶת־הַשָּׁמַיִם וְאֶת־הָאָרֶץ הַחַיִּים וְהַמָּוֶת נָתַתִּי
לְפָנֶיךָ הַבְּרָכָה וְהַקְּלָלָה וּבָחַרְתָּ בַּחַיִּים לְמַעַן תִּחְיֶה אַתָּה וְזַרְעֶךָ׃

Translating the Torah Study Text

Following is our Torah Study Text, Deuteronomy 30:11–16 and 19, reprinted with a literal translation underneath each word. Using your knowledge of the building blocks of the Hebrew language and the meanings of the words provided below, translate this passage into clear English sentences. Write your translation on the lines following the text. This selection includes some grammatical forms and vocabulary that have not yet been introduced. You will need to rely, in part, on the translations provided.

Deuteronomy 30:11–16

כִּי	הַמִּצְוָה הַזֹּאת	אֲשֶׁר	אָנֹכִי	מְצַוְּךָ	הַיּוֹם	לֹא־	נִפְלֵאת	הִוא
for	*this commandment*	*that*	*I*	*command you*	*today*	*not*	*extraordinary*	*it*

מִמְּךָ	וְלֹא־	רְחֹקָה	הִוא׃	לֹא	בַשָּׁמַיִם	הִוא	לֵאמֹר	מִי
from you	*and not*	*distant/ far*	*it*	*not*	*in the heaven/s*	*it*	*saying/ to say*	*who*

יַעֲלֶה־	לָּנוּ	הַשָּׁמַיְמָה	וְיִקָּחֶהָ	לָּנוּ	וְיַשְׁמִעֵנוּ	אֹתָהּ
will/may go up	*for us*	*heavenward*	*and take it*	*for us*	*and cause us to hear*	*it*

וְנַעֲשֶׂנָּה׃	וְלֹא־	מֵעֵבֶר	לַיָּם	הִוא	לֵאמֹר	מִי
so we may do it	*and not*	*from across/ beyond*	*the sea*	*it*	*saying/ to say*	*who*

יַעֲבָר־	לָנוּ	אֶל־	עֵבֶר	הַיָּם	וְיִקָּחֶהָ	לָּנוּ
will/may cross	*for us*	*to*	*across/beyond*	*the sea*	*and take it*	*for us*

וְיַשְׁמִעֵנוּ	אֹתָהּ	וְנַעֲשֶׂנָּה:	כִּי־	קָרוֹב	אֵלֶיךָ	הַדָּבָר	מְאֹד
and cause us to hear	*it*	*so we may do it*	*for*	*near*	*to you*	*the word/ thing*	*very*

בְּפִיךָ	וּבִלְבָבְךָ	לַעֲשֹׂתוֹ:	רְאֵה	נָתַתִּי	לְפָנֶיךָ	הַיּוֹם
in your mouth	*and in your heart*	*to do it*	*see*	*I have given/set*	*before you*	*today*

אֶת־הַחַיִּים	וְאֶת־הַטּוֹב	וְאֶת־ הַמָּוֶת	וְאֶת־הָרָע:	אֲשֶׁר	אָנֹכִי
the life	*and the good*	*and the death*	*and the evil*	*that*	*I*

מְצַוְּךָ	הַיּוֹם	לְאַהֲבָה	אֶת־יְהוָֹה	אֱלֹהֶיךָ	לָלֶכֶת	בִּדְרָכָיו
command you	*today*	*to love*	*the Eternal*	*your God*	*to walk*	*in his ways*

וְלִשְׁמֹר	מִצְוֹתָיו	וְחֻקֹּתָיו	וּמִשְׁפָּטָיו
and to keep	*his commandments*	*and his statutes/ ordinances*	*and his judgments/ laws*

וְחָיִיתָ	וְרָבִיתָ	וּבֵרַכְךָ	יְהוָֹה	אֱלֹהֶיךָ
and you shall/ may live	*and increase/ multiply*	*and will/may bless you*	*the Eternal*	*your God*

בָּאָרֶץ	אֲשֶׁר־	אַתָּה	בָא־	שָׁמָּה	לְרִשְׁתָּהּ:
in the land	*that*	*you*	*come*	*to there*	*to possess it*

Deuteronomy 30:19

הַחַיִּים	וְאֶת־הָאָרֶץ		אֶת־הַשָּׁמַיִם	הַיּוֹם	בָכֶם	הַעִדֹתִי
the life	*the earth*	*and*	*the heaven/s*	*today*	*against you*	*I call as witness*

וְהַקְּלָלָה	הַבְּרָכָה	לְפָנֶיךָ	נָתַתִּי	וְהַמָּוֶת
and the curse	*the blessing*	*before you*	*I have given/set*	*and the death*

וְזַרְעֶךָ׃	אַתָּה	תִּחְיֶה	לְמַעַן	בַּחַיִּים	וּבָחַרְתָּ
and your offspring/seed	*you*	*you shall/ may live*	*so that*	*the life*	*so you shall/ may choose*

TORAH Translations

Compare your translation of Deuteronomy 30:11–16, 19 with the Torah translations below.

*11Surely, this Instruction which I enjoin upon you this day is not too
baffling for you, nor is it beyond reach. 12It is not in the heavens, that you should
say, "Who among us can go up to the heavens and get it for us and impart it to us, that
we may observe it?" 13Neither is it beyond the sea, that you should say, "Who among
us can cross to the other side of the sea and get it for us and impart it to us, that we
may observe it?" 14No, the thing is very close to you, in your mouth and in your heart,
to observe it.*

*15See, I set before you this day life and prosperity, death and adversity. 16For I com-
mand you this day, to love the LORD your God, to walk in His ways, and to keep His
commandments, His laws, and His rules, that you may thrive and increase, and that
the LORD your God may bless you in the land that you are about to enter and possess.... 19I call heaven and earth to witness against you this day: I have put before you
life and death, blessing and curse. Choose life—if you and your offspring would live....*

JPS HEBREW-ENGLISH TANAKH: THE TRADITIONAL HEBREW TEXT AND THE NEW JPS TRANSLATION—2D ED. PHILADELPHIA: JEWISH PUBLICATION SOCIETY, 1999.

*11For this commandment that I command you today—it is not hidden from you and it
is not distant. 12It is not in heaven, [for you] to say, "Who can ascend to the heaven for*

us and take it for us, so that we can listen to it and perform it?" [13]Nor is it across the
sea, [for you] to say, "Who can cross to the other side of the sea for us and take it for
us, so that we can listen to it and perform it?" [14]Rather, the matter is very near to
you—in your mouth and your heart—to perform it.

[15]See—I have placed before you today the life and the good, and the death and the
evil, [16]that which I command you today, to love HASHEM, your God, to walk in His
ways, to observe His commandments, His decrees, and His ordinances; then you will
live and you will multiply, and HASHEM, your God, will bless you in the Land to which
you come, to possess it.... [19]I call heaven and earth today to bear witness against you: I
have placed life and death before you, blessing and curse; and you shall choose life, so
that you will live, you and your offspring....

THE CHUMASH, ARTSCROLL SERIES, STONE EDITION. BROOKLYN: MESORAH PUBLICATIONS, 1993.

[11]For the commandment that I command you this day:
it is not too extraordinary for you,
it is not too far away!
[12]It is not in the heavens,
(for you) to say:
Who will go up for us to the heavens and get it for us
and have us hear it, that we may observe it?
[13]And it is not across the sea,
(for you) to say:
Who will cross for us, across the sea, and get it for us
and have us hear it, that we may observe it?
[14]Rather, near to you is the word, exceedingly,
in your mouth and in your heart, to observe it!
[15]See, I set before you today
life and good, and death and ill:
[16]in that I command you today
to love YHWH your God,
to walk in his ways
and to keep his commandments, his laws and his regulations,
that you may stay-alive and become many-more
and YHWH your God may bless you
in the land that you are entering to possess....

[19]I call-as-witness against you today the heavens and the earth:

life and death I place before you, blessing and curse;
now choose life, in order that you may stay-alive, you and your seed....

THE FIVE BOOKS OF MOSES: A NEW TRANSLATION WITH INTRODUCTIONS, COMMENTARY, AND NOTES BY EVERETT FOX. NEW YORK: SCHOCKEN BOOKS, 1995.

For this commandment which I command thee this day, it is not hidden from thee, neither is it far off. It is not in heaven, that thou shouldst say, Who shall go up for us to heaven, and bring it to us, that we may hear it, and do it? Nor is it beyond the sea, that thou shouldst say, Who shall go over the sea for us, and bring it to us, that we may hear it, and do it? But the word is very near to thee, in thy mouth, and in thy heart, that thou mayst do it. See, I have set before thee this day life and good, and death and evil; in that I command thee this day to love the LORD *thy* GOD*, to walk in his ways, and to keep his commandments and his statutes and his judgments: then thou shalt live and multiply: and the* LORD *thy* GOD *shall bless thee in the land into which thou goest to possess it....I call heaven and earth to witness this day against you, that I have set before thee life and death, blessing and cursing: therefore, choose life, that both thou and thy seed may live....*

THE JERUSALEM BIBLE, PUBLISHED FOR THE NAHUM ZEEV WILLIAMS FAMILY FOUNDATION AT HECHAL SHLOMO, JERUSALEM. JERUSALEM: KOREN PUBLISHERS JERUSALEM LTD., 1969.

Vocabulary

Locate each of the following words in the Torah Study Text: Deuteronomy 30:11–16,19.

today	—	הַיּוֹם
near, close	—	קָרוֹב
before	—	לִפְנֵי
death *m*	—	מָוֶת
evil *m*	—	רַע

Notes on the Vocabulary

1. Depending on the context, the word הַיּוֹם can mean "today" or "the day."
2. As with other adjectives, the word קָרוֹב has four forms:

   קְרוֹבוֹת *f pl* קְרוֹבִים *m pl* קְרוֹבָה *f sg* קָרוֹב *m sg*

3. The word רַע can be the noun "evil" or an adjective meaning "evil," "bad," or "wicked." As an adjective, it has four forms:

   רָעוֹת *f pl* רָעִים *m pl* רָעָה *f sg* רַע *m sg*

THE ROOT ע־ב־ר

The root ע־ב־ר appears in the פָּעַל pattern with the basic meaning of "pass (over, through, by)" or "cross." In the הִפְעִיל pattern, it means "cause to pass (over, through, by)," "bring across," or "transport." The participle, perfect, and imperfect forms of the root ע־ב־ר in both the פָּעַל and הִפְעִיל patterns can be found in the verb charts in the back of the book.

The root ע־ב־ר appears three times in our Torah Study Text in verse 13:

and not from across/beyond the sea is it	—	וְלֹא־מֵעֵבֶר לַיָּם הִוא
saying/to say, "Who will/may cross for us	—	לֵאמֹר מִי יַעֲבָר־לָנוּ
to across/beyond the sea	—	אֶל־עֵבֶר הַיָּם

The following words, both ancient and modern, are derived from the root ע־ב־ר.

past, past tense	—	עָבָר
region across, beyond; side	—	עֵבֶר
Hebrew (one from the region beyond, the other side)	—	עִבְרִי
Hebrew *(the language)*	—	עִבְרִית
sin, transgression	—	עֲבֵרָה
sinner, transgressor, wrongdoer, delinquent	—	עֲבַרְיָן
juvenile delinquency	—	עֲבַרְיָנוּת הַנֹּעַר
ford, pass, passage; transit, transition	—	מַעֲבָר
ford; ferry; transit camp *(built in Israel for new immigrants)*	—	מַעְבָּרָה
traffic	—	תַּעֲבוּרָה
conductor, conveyer	—	מַעֲבִיר
ferryman	—	מַעְבּוֹרַאי
ferryboat; parting of hair	—	מַעְבֹּרֶת

The basic meaning of the root מ־ו־ת is "die." In the הִפְעִיל pattern, it means "cause to die," "kill," or "put to death." The participle, perfect, and imperfect forms of the root מ־ו־ת in both the פָּעַל and הִפְעִיל patterns can be found in the verb charts in the back of the book.

The root מ־ו־ת appears twice in our Torah Study Text as the noun מָוֶת, "death":

(verse 15)

and (the) death and (the) evil	—	וְאֶת־הַמָּוֶת וְאֶת־הָרָע

(verse 19)

(the) life and (the) death I have set before you	—	הַחַיִּים וְהַמָּוֶת נָתַתִּי לְפָנֶיךָ

The following words and expressions, both ancient and modern, are derived from the root מ־ו־ת. The middle root letter ו drops out or appears as the vowel וֹ or וּ in many words formed from this root.

death	—	מָוֶת
the angel of death	—	מַלְאַךְ הַמָּוֶת
capital crime	—	חֵטְא מָוֶת
death sentence	—	מִשְׁפַּט מָוֶת
grave (the gates of death)	—	שַׁעֲרֵי מָוֶת
death *(poetic term)*	—	מָוְתָה
mortality, death	—	תְּמוּתָה
killing	—	הֲמָתָה

TORAH Commentary

The last word of verse 14, לַעֲשֹׂתוֹ, "to do it," is somewhat awkward. The verse could have simply read:
כִּי־קָרוֹב אֵלֶיךָ הַדָּבָר מְאֹד בְּפִיךָ וּבִלְבָבְךָ,
"For very near to you is the word/thing, in your mouth and in your heart."
What extra nuance or meaning is added by the inclusion of the word לַעֲשֹׂתוֹ?

In your mouth and in your heart, that you may do it...*You do not fulfill your obligation by that which is in your mouth and in your heart. That which is in your mouth and your heart is for* you *to do.*

R. MENAHEM MENDL OF KOTSK, AS QUOTED IN *TORAH GEMS*, COMP. AHARON YAAKOV GREENBERG, TRANS. R. DR. SHMUEL HIMELSTEIN. TEL AVIV AND BROOKLYN: YAVNEH PUBLISHING HOUSE, CHEMED BOOKS, 1998.

The word הַיּוֹם, "today," is stated in both verses 15 and 19.

Why did Moses stress that he was placing these choices before the people today*? Perhaps this word's message is that each and every day of our lives, the same choices Moses described stand before us to be confronted anew.*

DERASH MOSHE, RABBI MOSHE FEINSTEIN'S COMMENTS ON THE TORAH, TRANS. RABBI AVROHOM YOSEIF ROSENBERG. BROOKLYN: MESORAH PUBLICATIONS LTD., 1994.

The verb וּבָחַרְתָּ, "choose," in verse 19 is a perfect verb with reversing *vav* attached. This gives it the meaning of an imperfect verb, which can indicate future tense, ongoing incompleted action, or action that is wished or urged. The following commentary understands this verb to carry all these implications.

"...the Torah imperative, וּבָחַרְתָּ בַּחַיִּים, "you shall choose life," *is a directive which is never-ending. We are to diligently choose life, constantly seeking ways for self-improvement." The greatest danger to one's spiritual development is stagnation. One either grows constantly, or he falls behind. On the road to spiritual ascension, inertia is tantamount to failure.*

THE MIRRER MASHGIACH, HORAV YECHEZKEL LEVINSTEIN, QUOTED IN *PENINIM ON THE TORAH*, BY RABBI A.L. SCHEINBAUM. CLEVELAND: PENINIM PUBLICATIONS, 2000.

Exercises

1. Make flash cards for each of the new vocabulary words and Hebrew roots introduced in this chapter, or use the flash card set published as a companion to this book. Review the cards to learn all of them.

2. Draw a line connecting each Hebrew word to its English translation. For some words, there can be more than one correct translation.

today	לִפְנֵי
death	רַע
near	הַיּוֹם
before	מָוֶת
close	קָרוֹב
evil	

3. On the left are plural forms of words introduced as vocabulary in this chapter. Draw a line connecting each plural word to its singular form. Translate both into English.

________________	רָעוֹת	קָרוֹב	________________
________________	קְרוֹבִים	קְרוֹבָה	________________
________________	קְרוֹבוֹת	רַע	________________
________________	רָעִים	רָעָה	________________

4. Read and translate the following groups of words.

________________	b. דֶּרֶךְ הַמָּוֶת	________________	a. לִפְנֵי מֹשֶׁה
________________	מוֹתִי	________________	לְפָנַי
________________	מוֹתָם	________________	לְפָנֶיךָ
________________	יוֹם מוֹתָהּ	________________	לְפָנָיו
________________	לִפְנֵי מוֹתוֹ	________________	לִפְנֵיכֶם

c. אוֹר קָרוֹב ________
אֶרֶץ קְרוֹבָה ________
עָרִים קְרוֹבוֹת ________
קָרוֹב יְיָ לַכֹּל ________
קָרוֹב לָנוּ הָאִישׁ ________

d. עַיִן הָרַע ________
לֵב רַע ________
מַעֲשֶׂה רַע ________
רוּחַ רָעָה ________
פָּנִים רָעִים ________

e. עַד הַיּוֹם ________
לִפְנֵי הַיּוֹם ________
אַחַר הַיּוֹם ________
כְּמוֹ הַיּוֹם ________
הִנֵּה הַיּוֹם ________

5. Identify the root of each of the following verbs and whether it is a perfect, imperfect, or participle form. Translate.

Verb	Root	Form	Translation
מֵתִים	________	________	________
עוֹבֵר	________	________	________
עוֹבְרוֹת	________	________	________
מַעֲבִיר	________	________	________
מֵמִית	________	________	________
אָמוּת	________	________	________
תָּמוּתוּ	________	________	________
תַּעַבְרוּ	________	________	________
תַּעֲבִירוּ	________	________	________
אֶעֱבֹר	________	________	________
אַעֲבִיר	________	________	________
הֶעֱבַרְתִּי	________	________	________

Translation	Form	Root	Verb
________	________	________	עָבַרְתָּ
________	________	________	הֵמִית
________	________	________	הֱמִיתוּ

EXTRA CREDIT

Not in Heaven

The practice of Judaism in our time, whether liberal or traditional, is the result of centuries of rabbinic interpretation of the Torah. The ability to reinterpret and reapply the teachings of Torah to new and unforseen circumstances (such as the destruction of the Temple in Jerusalem in the year 70 C.E. and the end of the sacrificial rite) has been a major factor in Jewish survival. Where does the authority to reinterpret the Torah originate? A famous talmudic passage cites a verse from this chapter's Torah Study Text, Deuteronomy 30:12, to indicate that this authority does not reside in heaven, but has been given to us by God.

It has been taught: On that day, Rabbi Eliezer used all the arguments in the world, but the Sages did not accept them. He said to them, "If the law is in accordance with me, let this carob tree prove it!" Then the carob tree was uprooted from its place 100 cubits—some say 400 cubits. They said to him, "No proof can be brought from a carob tree." He then said to them, "If the law is in accordance with me, let the stream of water prove it!" Then the stream of water flowed backwards. They said to him, "No proof can be brought from a stream of water." He then said to them, "If the law is in accordance with me, let the walls of the house of study prove it!" The walls of the house of study leaned in, about to fall. Rabbi Yehoshua rebuked them, saying to them, "If scholars argue with one another about the law, what business is it of yours?" The walls did not fall, out of respect for Rabbi Yehoshua, and they did not become upright, out of respect for Rabbi Eliezer, and they are still standing inclined. Rabbi Eliezer then said to the Sages, "If the law is in accordance with me, let it be proved from heaven!" And a heavenly voice came forth and said, "Why are you disputing with Rabbi Eliezer when the law is in accordance with him in every case!" Rabbi Yehoshua stood upon his feet and said, "לֹא בַשָּׁמַיִם הִיא, It is not in heaven!" *(Deuteronomy 30:12). What did he mean by "it is not in heaven"? Rabbi Yirmeyah said, "Since the Torah has been given at Mount Sinai, we do not pay attention to a heavenly voice, because You [God] have written at Mount Sinai in the Torah: "after the majority to incline" (Exodus 23:2).*

Rabbi Natan met the prophet Elijah. He asked him, "What did the blessed Holy One do at that moment?" Elijah said to him, "God smiled and said, 'My children have defeated Me! My children have defeated Me.'"

BAVA M'TZIA 59B

Torah Study Text: Vocabulary and Root Review

This Unit's Torah Study Text, Deuteronomy 30:11–16 and 19, is reprinted below, highlighting the new vocabulary words as well as the words formed from the new Hebrew roots introduced in Chapter 9. Read this passage again, recalling the meaning of each of the highlighted words or roots.

Deuteronomy 30:11–16

11 כִּי הַמִּצְוָה הַזֹּאת אֲשֶׁר אָנֹכִי מְצַוְּךָ **הַיּוֹם** לֹא־נִפְלֵאת הִוא מִמְּךָ
וְלֹא־רְחֹקָה הִוא׃ 12 לֹא בַשָּׁמַיִם הִוא לֵאמֹר מִי יַעֲלֶה־לָּנוּ הַשָּׁמַיְמָה
וְיִקָּחֶהָ לָּנוּ וְיַשְׁמִעֵנוּ אֹתָהּ וְנַעֲשֶׂנָּה׃ 13 וְלֹא־**מֵעֵבֶר** לַיָּם הִוא לֵאמֹר
מִי **יַעֲבָר**־לָנוּ אֶל־**עֵבֶר** הַיָּם וְיִקָּחֶהָ לָּנוּ וְיַשְׁמִעֵנוּ אֹתָהּ וְנַעֲשֶׂנָּה׃
14 כִּי־**קָרוֹב** אֵלֶיךָ הַדָּבָר מְאֹד בְּפִיךָ וּבִלְבָבְךָ לַעֲשֹׂתוֹ׃ 15 רְאֵה נָתַתִּי
לְפָנֶיךָ הַיּוֹם אֶת־הַחַיִּים וְאֶת־הַטּוֹב וְאֶת־הַ**מָּוֶת** וְאֶת־הָ**רָע**׃ 16 אֲשֶׁר
אָנֹכִי מְצַוְּךָ **הַיּוֹם** לְאַהֲבָה אֶת־יְהוָה אֱלֹהֶיךָ לָלֶכֶת בִּדְרָכָיו
וְלִשְׁמֹר מִצְוֹתָיו וְחֻקֹּתָיו וּמִשְׁפָּטָיו וְחָיִיתָ וְרָבִיתָ וּבֵרַכְךָ יְהוָה
אֱלֹהֶיךָ בָּאָרֶץ אֲשֶׁר־אַתָּה בָא־שָׁמָּה לְרִשְׁתָּהּ׃

Deuteronomy 30:19

הַעִדֹתִי בָכֶם **הַיּוֹם** אֶת־הַשָּׁמַיִם וְאֶת־הָאָרֶץ הַחַיִּים וְהַ**מָּוֶת** נָתַתִּי
לְפָנֶיךָ הַבְּרָכָה וְהַקְּלָלָה וּבָחַרְתָּ בַּחַיִּים לְמַעַן תִּחְיֶה אַתָּה וְזַרְעֶךָ׃

Building Blocks

אֲנַחְנוּ and אָנוּ Verb Forms

The Hebrew pronouns אֲנַחְנוּ and אָנוּ both mean "we" and are used for masculine and feminine subjects. In Hebrew, there are distinct אֲנַחְנוּ or אָנוּ perfect and imperfect verb forms.

Perfect Forms: The נוּ Ending

In Chapter 7 of *Aleph Isn't Enough*, we introduced the נוּ pronoun ending that means "us" or "our" when attached to nouns, prepositions, and some verb forms:

our God	—	אֱלֹהֵינוּ	**God**	—	אֱלֹהִים
on us	—	עָלֵינוּ	**on**	—	עַל
has sanctified us	—	קִדְּשָׁנוּ	**has sanctified**	—	קִדֵּשׁ

The נוּ ending is also used to indicate that a verb is a perfect "we," אָנוּ or אֲנַחְנוּ, form. This same ending is used with all the Hebrew verb patterns. Following are examples of perfect פָּעַל, פִּעֵל, and הִפְעִיל verbs with this ending attached. Remember that there are other ways that perfect verbs could be translated:

we ate	—	אָכַלְנוּ
we sanctified/made holy	—	קִדַּשְׁנוּ
we transported/brought across	—	הֶעֱבַרְנוּ

Although words such as קִדְּשָׁנוּ, "has sanctified us," and קִדַּשְׁנוּ, "we sanctified," look very similar, it is usually clear from the context whether a verb has a pronoun ending attached or is a perfect "we," אָנוּ or אֲנַחְנוּ, form.

Imperfect Forms: The נ Prefix

The prefix נ attached to a verb indicates that the verb is an imperfect אָנוּ or אֲנַחְנוּ, "we," form. This same prefix is used with all the Hebrew verb patterns. The vowels appearing under the prefix נ vary, depending on the verb pattern and root letters. Following are examples of פָּעַל, פִּעֵל, and הִפְעִיל verbs with this prefix attached. Remember that there are other ways that imperfect verbs can be translated:

we will say/let us say	—	נֹאמַר
we will sanctify/let us sanctify	—	נְקַדֵּשׁ
we will transport	—	נַעֲבִיר

Torah Study Text with Building Blocks

Following is an excerpt, Deuteronomy 30:12–13, from this unit's Torah Study Text, reprinted with the two אָנוּ or אֲנַחְנוּ, "we," verbs highlighted. Reread these verses, noting that words with the pronoun נוּ ending are not highlighted. A translation is provided below for only the highlighted verbs. Remember that there could be other possible translations. For a full translation of these verses, refer back to Chapter 9.

Deuteronomy 30:12–13

12 לֹא בַשָּׁמַיִם הִוא לֵאמֹר מִי יַעֲלֶה־לָּנוּ הַשָּׁמַיְמָה וְיִקָּחֶהָ לָּנוּ
וְיַשְׁמִעֵנוּ אֹתָהּ **וְנַעֲשֶׂנָּה׃** 13 וְלֹא־מֵעֵבֶר לַיָּם הִוא לֵאמֹר מִי
יַעֲבָר־לָנוּ אֶל־עֵבֶר הַיָּם וְיִקָּחֶהָ לָּנוּ וְיַשְׁמִעֵנוּ אֹתָהּ **וְנַעֲשֶׂנָּה׃**

נַעֲשֶׂנָּה — **we may do it (נַעֲשֶׂה, we may do, *with* ◌ָהּ, it, *ending attached*)**

Grammar Enrichment

Perfect and Imperfect Forms of אָנוּ and אֲנַחְנוּ

The following charts include the "we," אָנוּ or אֲנַחְנוּ, forms in the perfect and imperfect for all the roots introduced in this book and in *Bet Is for B'reishit*. פָּעַל, פִּעֵל, and הִפְעִיל verb patterns are included. These are presented for enrichment only. It is not necessary to memorize the information on these charts.

The same variations noted earlier also appear here: When the final root letter is ה, the ה drops out in the perfect forms. When the middle root letter is ו, the ו drops out in the perfect forms. In many roots that begin with the letters י or נ, those letters drop out in the imperfect forms.

פָּעַל Verbs

Imperfect	Perfect	Root	Meaning
נֹאמַר	אָמַרְנוּ	א־מ־ר	say
נָבוֹא	בָּאנוּ	ב־ו־א	come
נִבְנֶה	בָּנִינוּ	ב־נ־ה	build
נִהְיֶה	הָיִינוּ	ה־י־ה	be
נֵלֵךְ	הָלַכְנוּ	ה־ל־ך	walk, go

נֵדַע	יָדַעְנוּ	י־ד־ע	know
נִירָא	יָרֵאנוּ	י־ר־א	fear, be in awe
נֵשֵׁב	יָשַׁבְנוּ	י־שׁ־ב	sit, dwell
נִקַּח	לָקַחְנוּ	ל־ק־ח	take
נָמוּת	מַתְנוּ	מ־ו־ת	die
נָנוּחַ	נַחְנוּ	נ־ו־ח	rest
נִשָּׂא	נָשָׂאנוּ	נ־שׂ־א	lift, bear, carry
נַעֲבֹד	עָבַדְנוּ	ע־ב־ד	work, serve
נַעֲבֹר	עָבַרְנוּ	ע־ב־ר	pass, cross
נַעֲלֶה	עָלִינוּ	ע־ל־ה	go up, ascend
נַעֲמֹד	עָמַדְנוּ	ע־מ־ד	stand
נִרְאֶה	רָאִינוּ	ר־א־ה	see

פִּעֵל Verbs

Imperfect	Perfect	Root	Meaning
נְבָרֵךְ	בֵּרַכְנוּ	ב־ר־ך	bless
נְדַבֵּר	דִּבַּרְנוּ	ד־ב־ר	speak, talk
נְהַלֵּל	הִלַּלְנוּ	ה־ל־ל	praise
נְחַיֶּה	חִיִּינוּ	ח־י־ה	bring to life
נְכַבֵּד	כִּבַּדְנוּ	כ־ב־ד	honor, respect
נְצַוֶּה	צִוִּינוּ	צ־ו־ה	command, order
נְקַדֵּשׁ	קִדַּשְׁנוּ	ק־ד־שׁ	make holy

הִפְעִיל Verbs

Imperfect	Perfect	Root	Meaning
נוֹלִיךְ	הוֹלַכְנוּ	ה־ל־ך	cause to go, lead, conduct
נַחֲיֶה	הֶחֱיִינוּ	ח־י־ה	keep alive
נוֹדִיעַ	הוֹדַעְנוּ	י־ד־ע	make known, announce
נוֹצִיא	הוֹצֵאנוּ	י־צ־א	cause to go out, bring out

נוֹשִׁיב	הוֹשַׁבְנוּ	י־שׁ־ב	cause to sit *or* dwell, seat
נָמִית	הֲמַתְנוּ	מ־ו־ת	cause to die, kill, put to death
נָנִיחַ	הֲנַחְנוּ	נ־ו־ח	cause to rest, pacify, calm
נַעֲבִיד	הֶעֱבַדְנוּ	ע־ב־ד	put to work, employ
נַעֲבִיר	הֶעֱבַרְנוּ	ע־ב־ר	cause to pass, bring across
נַעֲלֶה	הֶעֱלִינוּ	ע־ל־ה	cause to ascend, bring up
נַעֲמִיד	הֶעֱמַדְנוּ	ע־מ־ד	cause to stand, establish
נַרְאֶה	הֶרְאִינוּ	ר־א־ה	cause to see, show

An Additional Note on Hebrew Verb Patterns

We have introduced the פָּעַל, פִּעֵל, and הִפְעִיל verb patterns. There are other Hebrew verb patterns. One of these is the נִפְעַל *(nifal)* pattern, which we mention here without formally presenting, because it has a נ prefix in all forms of the participle and perfect tense. It is usually possible to tell from the context whether a verb is a נִפְעַל participle/perfect tense form or an imperfect "we," אֲנַחְנוּ\אָנוּ, form. Verbs in the נִפְעַל pattern often, though not always, have a passive meaning. The following examples of נִפְעַל verbs come from well-known prayers:

אֲדוֹן עוֹלָם

was created	—	נִבְרָא	***root meaning*** **create**	—	ב־ר־א
was made	—	נַעֲשָׂה	***root meaning*** **make**	—	ע־שׂ־ה
was called	—	נִקְרָא	***root meaning*** **call**	—	ק־ר־א

Lord/ruler of eternity/universe who reigned	אֲדוֹן עוֹלָם אֲשֶׁר מָלַךְ
before every creature was created	בְּטֶרֶם כָּל־יְצִיר נִבְרָא
when all was made by His {God's} wish	לְעֵת נַעֲשָׂה בְחֶפְצוֹ כֹּל
then sovereign/king His {God's} name was called.	אֲזַי מֶלֶךְ שְׁמוֹ נִקְרָא.

וְנֶאֱמַר

(it) was said/has been said	—	נֶאֱמַר	*root meaning* say	—	א־מ־ר

וְנֶאֱמַר, וְהָיָה יְיָ לְמֶלֶךְ עַל־כָּל־הָאָרֶץ, בַּיּוֹם הַהוּא יִהְיֶה יְיָ אֶחָד
וּשְׁמוֹ אֶחָד:

And it has been said: "The Eternal will be King/Sovereign over all the earth, on that day the Eternal will be One and His {God's} name One.

Additional Reading and Translation Practice

Translate the following excerpts from the Bible, prayer book, and Haggadah, using the extra vocabulary words provided. Check your translations against the English translations that follow.

1. From גְּבוּרוֹת—The second blessing of the *Amidah* is included in weekday, Shabbat, and festival services. The following line contains a הִפְעִיל participle form of the root מ־ו־ת.

master (of), possessor (of)	—	בַּעַל
resembles, is like	—	דּוֹמֶה לְ־
causing to sprout, making grow	—	מַצְמִיחַ
salvation	—	יְשׁוּעָה

מִי כָמוֹךְ בַּעַל גְּבוּרוֹת וּמִי דּוֹמֶה לָּךְ, מֶלֶךְ מֵמִית וּמְחַיֶּה
וּמַצְמִיחַ יְשׁוּעָה?

____

____

2. From the קְדוּשָּׁה—This passage is from the morning and afternoon weekday *Amidah*. The opening line contains both an imperfect אֲנַחְנוּ, "we," form and a הִפְעִיל participle form from the root ק־ד־שׁ.

just as, in the same way as	—	כְּשֵׁם שֶׁ־
word-pair form of שָׁמַיִם	—	שְׁמֵי
height	—	מָרוֹם

נְקַדֵּשׁ אֶת־שִׁמְךָ בָּעוֹלָם, כְּשֵׁם שֶׁמַּקְדִּישִׁים אוֹתוֹ בִּשְׁמֵי מָרוֹם...

---

3. עֲבָדִים הָיִינוּ—This passage is from the Passover Haggadah. The first two words of this line have been included in a song, often sung at Passover seders, also presented below. A perfect אֲנַחְנוּ, "we," form of the root ה־י־ה appears.

Pharoah — פַּרְעֹה

עֲבָדִים הָיִינוּ לְפַרְעֹה בְּמִצְרָיִם.

Song

now — עַתָּה

free (*literally:* sons/children of free men/people) — בְּנֵי חוֹרִין

עֲבָדִים הָיִינוּ, הָיִינוּ
עַתָּה בְּנֵי חוֹרִין, בְּנֵי חוֹרִין.

---

4. Psalm 137:1—This biblical verse has been given various musical settings, including a round in Hebrew and a reggae tune in English. Perfect אֲנַחְנוּ, "we," forms of the roots י־שׁ־ב and ב־כ־ה (cry, weep) appear.

rivers — נַהֲרוֹת

Babylon — בָּבֶל

also, even — גַּם

cry, weep — ב־כ־ה

in our remembrance of {as we remembered} — בְּזָכְרֵנוּ

עַל נַהֲרוֹת בָּבֶל שָׁם יָשַׁבְנוּ גַּם־בָּכִינוּ בְּזָכְרֵנוּ אֶת־צִיּוֹן:

---

5. Psalm 118:26—The first four words of this biblical verse are included in circumcision and wedding ceremonies. The entire verse is used as an invocation or among the welcoming words of blessing at various occasions. A perfect אֲנַחְנוּ, "we," form of the root ב־ר־ךְ appears.

participle from the root ב־ו־א (come) *used as a noun*	—	בָּא
בֵּרַכְנוּ *with* כֶם, "you" *ending*	—	בֵּרַכְנוּכֶם

בָּרוּךְ הַבָּא בְּשֵׁם יְהוָה, בֵּרַכְנוּכֶם מִבֵּית יְהוָה:

---

6. From בִּרְכַּת הַמָּזוֹן—Following is the opening statement from the Blessing after Meals, in which a leader invites those who have eaten to join in blessing. The imperfect אֲנַחְנוּ, "we," form of the root ב־ר־ךְ appears. Perfect אֲנַחְנוּ, "we," forms of the roots א־כ־ל and ח־י־ה appear.

friend	—	חָבֵר
let [it] be (*imperfect form of the verb* ה־י־ה, be)	—	יְהִי
blessed	—	מְבֹרָךְ
now	—	עַתָּה
permission	—	רְשׁוּת
company, group	—	חֶבְרָה
goodness	—	טוּב

Leader: חֲבֵרִים וַחֲבֵרוֹת נְבָרֵךְ!

Group: יְהִי שֵׁם יְיָ מְבֹרָךְ מֵעַתָּה וְעַד עוֹלָם.

Leader: יְהִי שֵׁם יְיָ מְבֹרָךְ מֵעַתָּה וְעַד עוֹלָם. בִּרְשׁוּת הַחֶבְרָה,

---

נְבָרֵךְ אֱלֹהֵינוּ שֶׁאָכַלְנוּ מִשֶּׁלּוֹ.

Group: בָּרוּךְ אֱלֹהֵינוּ שֶׁאָכַלְנוּ מִשֶּׁלּוֹ וּבְטוּבוֹ חָיִינוּ.

Leader: בָּרוּךְ אֱלֹהֵינוּ שֶׁאָכַלְנוּ מִשֶּׁלּוֹ וּבְטוּבוֹ חָיִינוּ.

Group: בָּרוּךְ הוּא וּבָרוּךְ שְׁמוֹ.

Translations

1. From גְּבוּרוֹת—Who is like You, Master/Possessor of strengths and who resembles You, Sovereign/King causing death and bringing life and making salvation grow?
2. From the קְדוּשָּׁה—We will/shall/may sanctify/make holy {Let us/May we sanctify/make holy} Your name in the world/universe just as they make it holy in heavens of height {the high heavens}...
3. עֲבָדִים הָיִינוּ—Slaves we were/had been to Pharoah in Egypt. *or* We were Pharoah's slaves in Egypt.

   Song: Slaves we were, we were. Now [we are] free, free.
4. Psalm 137:1—Upon {by} the rivers of Babylon, there we sat/did sit/were sitting/had sat, also/even we wept/did weep/were weeping/had wept in our remembrance of {as we remembered} Zion.
5. Psalm 118:26—Blessed is the one who comes in the name of the Eternal, we bless/did bless/have blessed you from the house of the Eternal.
6. From בִּרְכַּת הַמָּזוֹן—

   Leader: Friends *(male)* and friends *(female)*, let us bless {may we bless, we may/will/shall bless}!

   Group: Let the name of the Eternal be blessed from now and unto eternity.

   Leader: Let the name of the Eternal be blessed from now and unto eternity. With the permission of the company/group, let us bless {may we bless, we may/will/shall bless} our God that we ate/did eat/have eaten from that which is His {God's}.

   Group: Blessed is our God that we ate/did eat/have eaten from that which is His {God's} and with His {God's} goodness, we have lived.

   Leader: Blessed is our God that we ate/did eat/have eaten from that which is His {God's} and with His {God's} goodness, we have lived.

   Group: Blessed is He {God} and blessed is His {God's} name.

Exercises

1. Identify the root of each of the following verbs and whether it is a perfect or imperfect form. Translate.

Translation	Form	Root	Verb
______	______	______	נַעֲלֶה
______	______	______	נִבְחַר
______	______	______	עָזַרְנוּ
______	______	______	בָּנִינוּ
______	______	______	יָדַעְנוּ
______	______	______	נֵלֵךְ
______	______	______	נְדַבֵּר
______	______	______	נְהַלֵּל
______	______	______	רָפָאנוּ
______	______	______	נַעֲמֹד
______	______	______	נִקַּח
______	______	______	נִירָא
______	______	______	הֶחֱיִינוּ
______	______	______	נוֹצִיא
______	______	______	נָמוּת

2. In each of the following phrases or sentences, circle the one form in the parentheses that is grammatically correct. Translate.

a. יֵשׁ לָנוּ בַּת (אַחַת, רַע, הַגְּדוֹלִים). ______________________

____

b. הָלַכְנוּ אֶל הַמָּקוֹם (קָדוֹשׁ, הַקָּרוֹב, אַחֶרֶת). ______________________

____

c. רָאִינוּ אֶת אַחֵינוּ (חוֹלוֹת, גִּבּוֹר, הַחוֹלִים). ______________________

____

d. נָנוּחַ קָרוֹב לַשַּׁעַר (הָאַחֵר, גְּדוֹלָה, קְדוֹשִׁים). ______________________

____

e. נְכַבֵּד נָשִׁים (רָעִים, רַבּוֹת, אֶחָד) בְּתוֹךְ הָעֵדָה. ______________________

____

f. אָנוּ נוֹתְנִים נֵר בַּחֹשֶׁךְ לְרֵעֵינוּ (קְדוֹשָׁה, הַטּוֹבִים, גִּבּוֹר). ______________________

____

3. Read and translate the following groups of sentences. Remember that the prefix *vav* can indicate a reverse verb tense. Check your translations against those that follow.

a. עָבַרְנוּ לִפְנֵי הַכֹּהֵן כַּאֲשֶׁר דִּבַּרְנוּ. ______________________

____

נַעֲבֹר לְפָנָיו כַּאֲשֶׁר דִּבַּרְתָּ. ______________________

____

לֹא נַעֲבֹר אֶת הַמִּדְבָּר כִּי אֵין לָנוּ מַיִם. ______________________

____

לֹא נַעֲבִיר אֶת מִשְׁפְּחוֹתֵינוּ מִן הֶהָרִים. ______________________

____

b. וַיְבָרֶךְ אָבִינוּ אֶת כָּל זֶרַע בֵּיתוֹ לִפְנֵי מוֹתוֹ. ______________________

____

וַתְּבָרֶךְ אִמֵּנוּ אֶת כָּל זֶרַע בֵּיתָהּ לִפְנֵי מוֹתָהּ. ______________________

____

נְבָרֵךְ אֶת בָּנֵינוּ וּבְנוֹתֵינוּ לִפְנֵי יוֹם מוֹתֵנוּ. ______________________

____

נְבָרֵךְ אוֹתָם בְּעֶרֶב שַׁבָּת.

c. וַיֹּאמֶר מַלְאַךְ הַמָּוֶת: הַיּוֹם תָּמוּת!

וַיֹּאמֶר הָאָדָם: אַל תְּמִיתֵנִי! תָּמִית אִישׁ אַחֵר!

וַיֹּאמֶר הַמַּלְאָךְ: בָּאתִי לְךָ הַיּוֹם וְלֹא לְאִישׁ אַחֵר.

לְכָל אִישׁ יֵשׁ יוֹם הַמָּוֶת.

d. נִשָּׂא אֲבָנִים לַגֵּרִים אֲשֶׁר אֵין לָהֶם בָּתִּים.

נִבְנֶה לָהֶם בָּתִּים, אֲנַחְנוּ וּנְעָרֵינוּ.

נַאֲכִילֵם וְנַעְזְרֵם.

וְיֵשְׁבוּ בְּתוֹכֵנוּ בְּשָׁלוֹם וְלֹא נִירָא.

Translations

a. We passed/did pass/were passing/had passed/have passed before the priest as/when we spoke/did speak/were speaking/had spoken/have spoken.

We will/shall/may pass {Let us/May we pass} before him as you spoke/did speak/had spoken.

We will/shall/may not cross {Let us not cross/May we not cross} the desert/wilderness because there is not to us {we do not have} water.

We will/shall/may not transport {Let us not transport} our families from the mountains.

b. Our father blessed/did bless all his offspring before his death.

Our mother blessed/did bless all her offspring before her death.

We will/shall/may {May we/Let us} bless our sons and our daughters before the day of our death.

We will/shall/may {May we/Let us} bless them in {on} the evening of Shabbat.

c. The angel of death said/did say: "Today you shall/will die!"

The man/human being said: "Do not kill me {cause me to die}. May you kill {Cause to die} a different/another man!"

The angel said, "I came/did come/have come to/for you today and not to/for a different/another man."

For every man there is {Every man has} a day of [the] death.

d. We will/shall/may carry {Let us carry} stones to/for the strangers/sojourners that there are not to them houses {that do not have houses.}

We will/shall/may build {Let us build} for them houses, we and our lads/young men.

We will/shall/may feed {Let us feed} them and we will/shall/may help {let us help} them.

And they will/shall/may settle/dwell in our midst in peace and we shall/will/may not fear.

FROM OUR TEXTS

"Hava Nagila"

"Hava Nagila" has become one of the best known Hebrew folk songs. It is said that the tune originated in the Chasidic community of the Sadigura Rebbe, and was brought to Palestine in the early twentieth century. The text was composed by Moshe Nathanson.

At the celebrations of joyous life-cycle events such as weddings and *b'nei mitzvah,* "Hava Nagila" is the tune that generally gets everyone up to dance the hora. The words נָגִילָה וְנִשְׂמְחָה appear in Psalm 118:24. The words נָגִילָה, "let us rejoice," נִשְׂמְחָה, "let us be happy," and נְרַנְּנָה, "let us sing with joy" are all אֲנַחְנוּ, "we," forms.

Come, let us rejoice	הָבָה נָגִילָה *(3X)*
and let us be happy!	וְנִשְׂמְחָה
Come, let us sing with joy	הָבָה נְרַנְּנָה *(3X)*
and let us be happy!	וְנִשְׂמְחָה
Awaken, awaken brothers!	עוּרוּ, עוּרוּ אַחִים
Awaken brothers, with a happy heart!	עוּרוּ אַחִים בְּלֵב שָׂמֵחַ *(5X)*

A Concluding Thought

Mazal tov on all that you have accomplished in your study of Hebrew! While there always remains more to learn, you have attained a significant level of Hebrew knowledge and are to be commended for it.

In the Talmud, *Taanit* 7a, Rabbi Chanina is credited with saying, "Much have I learned from my teachers, more from my colleagues, but from my students most of all." We hope that you have enjoyed learning from your teachers and your study partners, and we encourage you to continue that learning in the future. As Rabbi Chanina indicates, our greatest learning often comes from those whom we teach. And so we also encourage you to consider offering your knowledge in your community as a Hebrew teacher, to share what you have learned with others who know less. It may prove to be the best reward for all your studies. May you go from strength to strength!

Verb Charts

The following charts contain all the verb roots, in Hebrew alphabetical order, introduced in *Aleph Isn't Enough, Bet Is for B'reishit*, and *Tav Is for Torah*. Variant forms of these verbs appear in the Bible and prayerbooks. The verb charts are separated according to verb pattern: פָּעַל, פִּעֵל, and הִפְעִיל. Within each verb pattern, they are separated according to perfect, participle, and imperfect forms. The אַתְּ (you *f sg*) and אַתֶּן (you *f pl*) forms were not introduced in the text because they appear very infrequently in the Bible and prayer book, but they are included in these charts.

פָּעַל Perfect

הֵם\הֵן they *m/f*	אַתֶּן you *f pl*	אַתֶּם you *m pl*	אֲנַחְנוּ we	הִיא she	הוּא he	אַתְּ you *f*	אַתָּה you *m*	אֲנִי I	Root	Meaning
אָהֲבוּ	אֲהַבְתֶּן	אֲהַבְתֶּם	אָהַבְנוּ	אָהֲבָה	אָהַב	אָהַבְתְּ	אָהַבְתָּ	אָהַבְתִּי	א־ה־ב	love
אָכְלוּ	אֲכַלְתֶּן	אֲכַלְתֶּם	אָכַלְנוּ	אָכְלָה	אָכַל	אָכַלְתְּ	אָכַלְתָּ	אָכַלְתִּי	א־כ־ל	eat
אָמְרוּ	אֲמַרְתֶּן	אֲמַרְתֶּם	אָמַרְנוּ	אָמְרָה	אָמַר	אָמַרְתְּ	אָמַרְתָּ	אָמַרְתִּי	א־מ־ר	say
בָּאוּ	בָּאתֶן	בָּאתֶם	בָּאנוּ	בָּאָה	בָּא	בָּאת	בָּאתָ	בָּאתִי	ב־ו־א	come
בָּחֲרוּ	בְּחַרְתֶּן	בְּחַרְתֶּם	בָּחַרְנוּ	בָּחֲרָה	בָּחַר	בָּחַרְתְּ	בָּחַרְתָּ	בָּחַרְתִּי	ב־ח־ר	choose
בָּנוּ	בְּנִיתֶן	בְּנִיתֶם	בָּנִינוּ	בָּנְתָה	בָּנָה	בָּנִית	בָּנִיתָ	בָּנִיתִי	ב־נ־ה	build
בָּרְאוּ	בְּרָאתֶן	בְּרָאתֶם	בָּרָאנוּ	בָּרְאָה	בָּרָא	בָּרָאת	בָּרָאתָ	בָּרָאתִי	ב־ר־א	create
הָיוּ	הֱיִיתֶן	הֱיִיתֶם	הָיִינוּ	הָיְתָה	הָיָה	הָיִית	הָיִיתָ	הָיִיתִי	ה־י־ה	be
הָלְכוּ	הֲלַכְתֶּן	הֲלַכְתֶּם	הָלַכְנוּ	הָלְכָה	הָלַךְ	הָלַכְתְּ	הָלַכְתָּ	הָלַכְתִּי	ה־ל־ך	walk, go
זָכְרוּ	זְכַרְתֶּן	זְכַרְתֶּם	זָכַרְנוּ	זָכְרָה	זָכַר	זָכַרְתְּ	זָכַרְתָּ	זָכַרְתִּי	ז־כ־ר	remember
יָדְעוּ	יְדַעְתֶּן	יְדַעְתֶּם	יָדַעְנוּ	יָדְעָה	יָדַע	יָדַעַתְּ	יָדַעְתָּ	יָדַעְתִּי	י־ד־ע	know
יָצְאוּ	יְצָאתֶן	יְצָאתֶם	יָצָאנוּ	יָצְאָה	יָצָא	יָצָאת	יָצָאתָ	יָצָאתִי	י־צ־א	go out

Meaning	Root	אֲנִי I	אַתָּה you m	אַתְּ you f	הוּא he	הִיא she	אֲנַחְנוּ we	אַתֶּם you m pl	אַתֶּן you f pl	הֵם\הֵן they m/f
fear, revere	י־ר־א	יָרֵאתִי	יָרֵאתָ	יָרֵאת	יָרֵא	יָרְאָה	יָרֵאנוּ	יְרֵאתֶם	יְרֵאתֶן	יָרְאוּ
sit, dwell	י־שׁ־ב	יָשַׁבְתִּי	יָשַׁבְתָּ	יָשַׁבְתְּ	יָשַׁב	יָשְׁבָה	יָשַׁבְנוּ	יְשַׁבְתֶּם	יְשַׁבְתֶּן	יָשְׁבוּ
take	ל־ק־ח	לָקַחְתִּי	לָקַחְתָּ	לָקַחַתְּ	לָקַח	לָקְחָה	לָקַחְנוּ	לְקַחְתֶּם	לְקַחְתֶּן	לָקְחוּ
die	מ־ו־ת	מַתִּי	מַתָּ	מַתְּ	מֵת	מֵתָה	מַתְנוּ	מַתֶּם	מַתֶּן	מֵתוּ
reign, rule	מ־ל־ך	מָלַכְתִּי	מָלַכְתָּ	מָלַכְתְּ	מָלַךְ	מָלְכָה	מָלַכְנוּ	מְלַכְתֶּם	מְלַכְתֶּן	מָלְכוּ
rest	נ־ו־ח	נַחְתִּי	נַחְתָּ	נַחְתְּ	נָח	נָחָה	נַחְנוּ	נַחְתֶּם	נַחְתֶּן	נָחוּ
lift, carry	נ־שׂ־א	נָשָׂאתִי	נָשָׂאתָ	נָשָׂאת	נָשָׂא	נָשְׂאָה	נָשָׂאנוּ	נְשָׂאתֶם	נְשָׂאתֶן	נָשְׂאוּ
give	נ־ת־ן	נָתַתִּי	נָתַתָּ	נָתַתְּ	נָתַן	נָתְנָה	נָתַנּוּ	נְתַתֶּם	נְתַתֶּן	נָתְנוּ
work, serve	ע־ב־ד	עָבַדְתִּי	עָבַדְתָּ	עָבַדְתְּ	עָבַד	עָבְדָה	עָבַדְנוּ	עֲבַדְתֶּם	עֲבַדְתֶּן	עָבְדוּ
pass, cross	ע־ב־ר	עָבַרְתִּי	עָבַרְתָּ	עָבַרְתְּ	עָבַר	עָבְרָה	עָבַרְנוּ	עֲבַרְתֶּם	עֲבַרְתֶּן	עָבְרוּ
help	ע־ז־ר	עָזַרְתִּי	עָזַרְתָּ	עָזַרְתְּ	עָזַר	עָזְרָה	עָזַרְנוּ	עֲזַרְתֶּם	עֲזַרְתֶּן	עָזְרוּ
go up	ע־ל־ה	עָלִיתִי	עָלִיתָ	עָלִית	עָלָה	עָלְתָה	עָלִינוּ	עֲלִיתֶם	עֲלִיתֶן	עָלוּ
stand	ע־מ־ד	עָמַדְתִּי	עָמַדְתָּ	עָמַדְתְּ	עָמַד	עָמְדָה	עָמַדְנוּ	עֲמַדְתֶּם	עֲמַדְתֶּן	עָמְדוּ
make, do	ע־שׂ־ה	עָשִׂיתִי	עָשִׂיתָ	עָשִׂית	עָשָׂה	עָשְׂתָה	עָשִׂינוּ	עֲשִׂיתֶם	עֲשִׂיתֶן	עָשׂוּ
see	ר־א־ה	רָאִיתִי	רָאִיתָ	רָאִית	רָאָה	רָאֲתָה	רָאִינוּ	רְאִיתֶם	רְאִיתֶן	רָאוּ
heal	ר־פ־א	רָפָאתִי	רָפָאתָ	רָפָאת	רָפָא	רָפְאָה	רָפָאנוּ	רְפָאתֶם	רְפָאתֶן	רָפְאוּ
hear	שׁ־מ־ע	שָׁמַעְתִּי	שָׁמַעְתָּ	שָׁמַעַתְּ	שָׁמַע	שָׁמְעָה	שָׁמַעְנוּ	שְׁמַעְתֶּם	שְׁמַעְתֶּן	שָׁמְעוּ
guard, keep	שׁ־מ־ר	שָׁמַרְתִּי	שָׁמַרְתָּ	שָׁמַרְתְּ	שָׁמַר	שָׁמְרָה	שָׁמַרְנוּ	שְׁמַרְתֶּם	שְׁמַרְתֶּן	שָׁמְרוּ

פָּעַל Participle

The following roots follow the exact same pattern as the regular root א־מ־ר and are not listed in the chart: א־כ־ל, ה־ל־ך, ז־כ־ר, י־ש־ב, מ־ל־ך, נ־ת־ן, ע־ב־ד, ע־ב־ר, ע־ז־ר, ע־מ־ד, and ש־מ־ר. There is no פָּעַל participle form of the root ה־י־ה.

Feminine Plural	Masculine Plural	Feminine Singular	Masculine Singular	Root	Meaning
אוֹהֲבוֹת	אוֹהֲבִים	אוֹהֶבֶת	אוֹהֵב	א־ה־ב	love
אוֹמְרוֹת	אוֹמְרִים	אוֹמֶרֶת	אוֹמֵר	א־מ־ר	say
בָּאוֹת	בָּאִים	בָּאָה	בָּא	ב־ו־א	come
בּוֹחֲרוֹת	בּוֹחֲרִים	בּוֹחֶרֶת	בּוֹחֵר	ב־ח־ר	choose
בּוֹנוֹת	בּוֹנִים	בּוֹנָה	בּוֹנֶה	ב־נ־ה	build
בּוֹרְאוֹת	בּוֹרְאִים	בּוֹרֵאת	בּוֹרֵא	ב־ר־א	create
יוֹדְעוֹת	יוֹדְעִים	יוֹדַעַת	יוֹדֵעַ	י־ד־ע	know
יוֹצְאוֹת	יוֹצְאִים	יוֹצֵאת	יוֹצֵא	י־צ־א	go out
יְרֵאוֹת	יְרֵאִים	יְרֵאָה	יָרֵא	י־ר־א	fear, revere
לוֹקְחוֹת	לוֹקְחִים	לוֹקַחַת	לוֹקֵחַ	ל־ק־ח	take
מֵתוֹת	מֵתִים	מֵתָה	מֵת	מ־ו־ת	die
נָחוֹת	נָחִים	נָחָה	נָח	נ־ו־ח	rest
נוֹשְׂאוֹת	נוֹשְׂאִים	נוֹשֵׂאת	נוֹשֵׂא	נ־שׂ־א	lift, carry
עוֹלוֹת	עוֹלִים	עוֹלָה	עוֹלֶה	ע־ל־ה	go up, ascend
עוֹשׂוֹת	עוֹשִׂים	עוֹשָׂה	עוֹשֶׂה	ע־שׂ־ה	make, do
רוֹאוֹת	רוֹאִים	רוֹאָה	רוֹאֶה	ר־א־ה	see
רוֹפְאוֹת	רוֹפְאִים	רוֹפֵאת	רוֹפֵא	ר־פ־א	heal
שׁוֹמְעוֹת	שׁוֹמְעִים	שׁוֹמַעַת	שׁוֹמֵעַ	שׁ־מ־ע	hear

פָּעַל Imperfect

הֵם they *m/f*	אַתֶּן, הֵן *you, they f pl*	אַתֶּם you *m pl*	אֲנַחְנוּ we	הִיא she	הוּא he	אַתְּ you *f*	אַתָּה you *m*	אֲנִי I	Root	Meaning
יֶאֱהֲבוּ	תֶּאֱהַבְנָה	תֶּאֱהֲבוּ	נֶאֱהַב	תֶּאֱהַב	יֶאֱהַב	תֶּאֱהֲבִי	תֶּאֱהַב	אֶאֱהַב	א־ה־ב	love
יֹאהֲבוּ	תֹּאהַבְנָה	תֹּאהֲבוּ	נֹאהַב	תֹּאהַב	יֹאהַב	תֹּאהֲבִי	תֹּאהַב	אֹהַב	א־ה־ב	love (alternate form)
יֹאכְלוּ	תֹּאכַלְנָה	תֹּאכְלוּ	נֹאכַל	תֹּאכַל	יֹאכַל	תֹּאכְלִי	תֹּאכַל	אֹכַל	א־כ־ל	eat
יֹאמְרוּ	תֹּאמַרְנָה	תֹּאמְרוּ	נֹאמַר	תֹּאמַר	יֹאמַר	תֹּאמְרִי	תֹּאמַר	אֹמַר	א־מ־ר	say
יָבוֹאוּ	תָּבֹאנָה	תָּבוֹאוּ	נָבוֹא	תָּבוֹא	יָבוֹא	תָּבוֹאִי	תָּבוֹא	אָבוֹא	ב־ו־א	come
יִבְחֲרוּ	תִּבְחַרְנָה	תִּבְחֲרוּ	נִבְחַר	תִּבְחַר	יִבְחַר	תִּבְחֲרִי	תִּבְחַר	אֶבְחַר	ב־ח־ר	choose
יִבְנוּ	תִּבְנֶינָה	תִּבְנוּ	נִבְנֶה	תִּבְנֶה	יִבְנֶה	תִּבְנִי	תִּבְנֶה	אֶבְנֶה	ב־נ־ה	build
יִבְרְאוּ	תִּבְרֶאנָה	תִּבְרְאוּ	נִבְרָא	תִּבְרָא	יִבְרָא	תִּבְרְאִי	תִּבְרָא	אֶבְרָא	ב־ר־א	create
יִהְיוּ	תִּהְיֶינָה	תִּהְיוּ	נִהְיֶה	תִּהְיֶה	יִהְיֶה	תִּהְיִי	תִּהְיֶה	אֶהְיֶה	ה־י־ה	be
יֵלְכוּ	תֵּלַכְנָה	תֵּלְכוּ	נֵלֵךְ	תֵּלֵךְ	יֵלֵךְ	תֵּלְכִי	תֵּלֵךְ	אֵלֵךְ	ה־ל־ך	go, walk
יִזְכְּרוּ	תִּזְכֹּרְנָה	תִּזְכְּרוּ	נִזְכֹּר	תִּזְכֹּר	יִזְכֹּר	תִּזְכְּרִי	תִּזְכֹּר	אֶזְכֹּר	ז־כ־ר	remember
יֵדְעוּ	תֵּדַעְנָה	תֵּדְעוּ	נֵדַע	תֵּדַע	יֵדַע	תֵּדְעִי	תֵּדַע	אֵדַע	י־ד־ע	know
יֵצְאוּ	תֵּצֶאנָה	תֵּצְאוּ	נֵצֵא	תֵּצֵא	יֵצֵא	תֵּצְאִי	תֵּצֵא	אֵצֵא	י־צ־א	go out
יִירְאוּ	תִּירֶאנָה	תִּירְאוּ	נִירָא	תִּירָא	יִירָא	תִּירְאִי	תִּירָא	אִירָא	י־ר־א	fear, revere
יֵשְׁבוּ	תֵּשַׁבְנָה	תֵּשְׁבוּ	נֵשֵׁב	תֵּשֵׁב	יֵשֵׁב	תֵּשְׁבִי	תֵּשֵׁב	אֵשֵׁב	י־שׁ־ב	sit, dwell
יִקְחוּ	תִּקַּחְנָה	תִּקְחוּ	נִקַּח	תִּקַּח	יִקַּח	תִּקְחִי	תִּקַּח	אֶקַּח	ל־ק־ח	take

פָּעַל **Imperfect** (Continued)

הֵם they *m/f*	אַתֶּן, הֵן *you, they f pl*	אַתֶּם you *m pl*	אֲנַחְנוּ we	הִיא she	הוּא he	אַתְּ you *f*	אַתָּה you *m*	אֲנִי I	Root	Meaning
יָמוּתוּ	תָּמֹתְנָה	תָּמוּתוּ	נָמוּת	תָּמוּת	יָמוּת	תָּמוּתִי	תָּמוּת	אָמוּת	מ־ו־ת	die
יִמְלְכוּ	תִּמְלֹכְנָה	תִּמְלְכוּ	נִמְלֹךְ	תִּמְלֹךְ	יִמְלֹךְ	תִּמְלְכִי	תִּמְלֹךְ	אֶמְלֹךְ	מ־ל־ך	reign, rule
יָנוּחוּ	תָּנַחְנָה	תָּנוּחוּ	נָנוּחַ	תָּנוּחַ	יָנוּחַ	תָּנוּחִי	תָּנוּחַ	אָנוּחַ	נ־ו־ח	rest
יִשְׂאוּ	תִּשֶּׂאנָה	תִּשְׂאוּ	נִשָּׂא	תִּשָּׂא	יִשָּׂא	תִּשְׂאִי	תִּשָּׂא	אֶשָּׂא	נ־שׂ־א	lift, carry
יִתְּנוּ	תִּתֵּנָּה	תִּתְּנוּ	נִתֵּן	תִּתֵּן	יִתֵּן	תִּתְּנִי	תִּתֵּן	אֶתֵּן	נ־ת־ן	give
יַעַבְדוּ	תַּעֲבֹדְנָה	תַּעַבְדוּ	נַעֲבֹד	תַּעֲבֹד	יַעֲבֹד	תַּעַבְדִי	תַּעֲבֹד	אֶעֱבֹד	ע־ב־ד	work, serve
יַעַבְרוּ	תַּעֲבֹרְנָה	תַּעַבְרוּ	נַעֲבֹר	תַּעֲבֹר	יַעֲבֹר	תַּעַבְרִי	תַּעֲבֹר	אֶעֱבֹר	ע־ב־ר	pass, cross
יַעַזְרוּ	תַּעֲזֹרְנָה	תַּעַזְרוּ	נַעֲזֹר	תַּעֲזֹר	יַעֲזֹר	תַּעַזְרִי	תַּעֲזֹר	אֶעֱזֹר	ע־ז־ר	help
יַעֲלוּ	תַּעֲלֶינָה	תַּעֲלוּ	נַעֲלֶה	תַּעֲלֶה	יַעֲלֶה	תַּעֲלִי	תַּעֲלֶה	אֶעֱלֶה	ע־ל־ה	go up
יַעַמְדוּ	תַּעֲמֹדְנָה	תַּעַמְדוּ	נַעֲמֹד	תַּעֲמֹד	יַעֲמֹד	תַּעַמְדִי	תַּעֲמֹד	אֶעֱמֹד	ע־מ־ד	stand
יַעֲשׂוּ	תַּעֲשֶׂינָה	תַּעֲשׂוּ	נַעֲשֶׂה	תַּעֲשֶׂה	יַעֲשֶׂה	תַּעֲשִׂי	תַּעֲשֶׂה	אֶעֱשֶׂה	ע־שׂ־ה	make, do
יִרְאוּ	תִּרְאֶינָה	תִּרְאוּ	נִרְאֶה	תִּרְאֶה	יִרְאֶה	תִּרְאִי	תִּרְאֶה	אֶרְאֶה	ר־א־ה	see
יִרְפְּאוּ	תִּרְפֶּאנָה	תִּרְפְּאוּ	נִרְפָּא	תִּרְפָּא	יִרְפָּא	תִּרְפְּאִי	תִּרְפָּא	אֶרְפָּא	ר־פ־א	heal
יִשְׁמְעוּ	תִּשְׁמַעְנָה	תִּשְׁמְעוּ	נִשְׁמַע	תִּשְׁמַע	יִשְׁמַע	תִּשְׁמְעִי	תִּשְׁמַע	אֶשְׁמַע	שׁ־מ־ע	hear
יִשְׁמְרוּ	תִּשְׁמֹרְנָה	תִּשְׁמְרוּ	נִשְׁמֹר	תִּשְׁמֹר	יִשְׁמֹר	תִּשְׁמְרִי	תִּשְׁמֹר	אֶשְׁמֹר	שׁ־מ־ר	guard, keep

פִּעֵל Perfect

הֵם\הֵן they m/f	אַתֶּן you f pl	אַתֶּם you m pl	אֲנַחְנוּ we	הִיא she	הוּא he	אַתְּ you f	אַתָּה you m	אֲנִי I	Root	Meaning
בֵּרְכוּ	בֵּרַכְתֶּן	בֵּרַכְתֶּם	בֵּרַכְנוּ	בֵּרְכָה	בֵּרֵךְ	בֵּרַכְתְּ	בֵּרַכְתָּ	בֵּרַכְתִּי	ב־ר־ך	bless
דִּבְּרוּ	דִּבַּרְתֶּן	דִּבַּרְתֶּם	דִּבַּרְנוּ	דִּבְּרָה	דִּבֵּר	דִּבַּרְתְּ	דִּבַּרְתָּ	דִּבַּרְתִּי	ד־ב־ר	speak
הִלְּלוּ	הִלַּלְתֶּן	הִלַּלְתֶּם	הִלַּלְנוּ	הִלְּלָה	הִלֵּל	הִלַּלְתְּ	הִלַּלְתָּ	הִלַּלְתִּי	ה־ל־ל	praise
חִיּוּ	חִיִּיתֶן	חִיִּיתֶם	חִיִּינוּ	חִיְּתָה	חִיָּה	חִיִּית	חִיִּיתָ	חִיִּיתִי	ח־י־ה	bring to life
כִּבְּדוּ	כִּבַּדְתֶּן	כִּבַּדְתֶּם	כִּבַּדְנוּ	כִּבְּדָה	כִּבֵּד	כִּבַּדְתְּ	כִּבַּדְתָּ	כִּבַּדְתִּי	כ־ב־ד	honor
צִוּוּ	צִוִּיתֶן	צִוִּיתֶם	צִוִּינוּ	צִוְּתָה	צִוָּה	צִוִּית	צִוִּיתָ	צִוִּיתִי	צ־ו־ה	command
קִדְּשׁוּ	קִדַּשְׁתֶּן	קִדַּשְׁתֶּם	קִדַּשְׁנוּ	קִדְּשָׁה	קִדֵּשׁ	קִדַּשְׁתְּ	קִדַּשְׁתָּ	קִדַּשְׁתִּי	ק־ד־ש	make holy

פִּעֵל Participle

Feminine Plural	*Masculine Plural*	*Feminine Singular*	*Masculine Singular*	Root	Meaning
מְבָרְכוֹת	מְבָרְכִים	מְבָרֶכֶת	מְבָרֵךְ	ב־ר־ך	bless
מְדַבְּרוֹת	מְדַבְּרִים	מְדַבֶּרֶת	מְדַבֵּר	ד־ב־ר	speak
מְהַלְלוֹת	מְהַלְלִים	מְהַלֶּלֶת	מְהַלֵּל	ה־ל־ל	praise
מְחַיּוֹת	מְחַיִּים	מְחַיָּה	מְחַיֶּה	ח־י־ה	bring to life
מְכַבְּדוֹת	מְכַבְּדִים	מְכַבֶּדֶת	מְכַבֵּד	כ־ב־ד	honor, respect
מְצַוּוֹת	מְצַוִּים	מְצַוָּה	מְצַוֶּה	צ־ו־ה	command, order
מְקַדְּשׁוֹת	מְקַדְּשִׁים	מְקַדֶּשֶׁת	מְקַדֵּשׁ	ק־ד־ש	make holy

פִּעֵל Imperfect

הֵם they m/f	אַתֶּן, הֵן you, they f pl	אַתֶּם you m pl	אֲנַחְנוּ we	הִיא she	הוּא he	אַתְּ you f	אַתָּה you m	אֲנִי I	Root	Meaning
יְבָרְכוּ	תְּבָרֵכְנָה	תְּבָרְכוּ	נְבָרֵךְ	תְּבָרֵךְ	יְבָרֵךְ	תְּבָרְכִי	תְּבָרֵךְ	אֲבָרֵךְ	ב־ר־ך	bless
יְדַבְּרוּ	תְּדַבֵּרְנָה	תְּדַבְּרוּ	נְדַבֵּר	תְּדַבֵּר	יְדַבֵּר	תְּדַבְּרִי	תְּדַבֵּר	אֲדַבֵּר	ד־ב־ר	speak
יְהַלְלוּ	תְּהַלֵּלְנָה	תְּהַלְלוּ	נְהַלֵּל	תְּהַלֵּל	יְהַלֵּל	תְּהַלְלִי	תְּהַלֵּל	אֲהַלֵּל	ה־ל־ל	praise
יְחַיּוּ	תְּחַיֶּינָה	תְּחַיּוּ	נְחַיֶּה	תְּחַיֶּה	יְחַיֶּה	תְּחַיִּי	תְּחַיֶּה	אֲחַיֶּה	ח־י־ה	bring to life
יְכַבְּדוּ	תְּכַבֵּדְנָה	תְּכַבְּדוּ	נְכַבֵּד	תְּכַבֵּד	יְכַבֵּד	תְּכַבְּדִי	תְּכַבֵּד	אֲכַבֵּד	כ־ב־ד	honor
יְצַוּוּ	תְּצַוֶּינָה	תְּצַוּוּ	נְצַוֶּה	תְּצַוֶּה	יְצַוֶּה	תְּצַוִּי	תְּצַוֶּה	אֲצַוֶּה	צ־ו־ה	command
יְקַדְּשׁוּ	תְּקַדֵּשְׁנָה	תְּקַדְּשׁוּ	נְקַדֵּשׁ	תְּקַדֵּשׁ	יְקַדֵּשׁ	תְּקַדְּשִׁי	תְּקַדֵּשׁ	אֲקַדֵּשׁ	ק־ד־שׁ	make holy

הִפְעִיל Perfect

הֵם\הֵן they m/f	אַתֶּן you f pl	אַתֶּם you m pl	אֲנַחְנוּ we	הִיא she	הוּא he	אַתְּ you f	אַתָּה you m	אֲנִי I	Root	Meaning
הֶאֱכִילוּ	הֶאֱכַלְתֶּן	הֶאֱכַלְתֶּם	הֶאֱכַלְנוּ	הֶאֱכִילָה	הֶאֱכִיל	הֶאֱכַלְתְּ	הֶאֱכַלְתָּ	הֶאֱכַלְתִּי	א־כ־ל	cause to eat, feed
הֶאֱמִינוּ	הֶאֱמַנְתֶּן	הֶאֱמַנְתֶּם	הֶאֱמַנּוּ	הֶאֱמִינָה	הֶאֱמִין	הֶאֱמַנְתְּ	הֶאֱמַנְתָּ	הֶאֱמַנְתִּי	א־מ־ן	trust, believe
הֵבִיאוּ	הֲבֵאתֶן	הֲבֵאתֶם	הֵבֵאנוּ	הֵבִיאָה	הֵבִיא	הֵבֵאת	הֵבֵאתָ	הֵבֵאתִי	ב־ו־א	cause to come, bring
הוֹלִיכוּ	הוֹלַכְתֶּן	הוֹלַכְתֶּם	הוֹלַכְנוּ	הוֹלִיכָה	הוֹלִיךְ	הוֹלַכְתְּ	הוֹלַכְתָּ	הוֹלַכְתִּי	ה־ל־ך	cause to go, lead, conduct
הִזְכִּירוּ	הִזְכַּרְתֶּן	הִזְכַּרְתֶּם	הִזְכַּרְנוּ	הִזְכִּירָה	הִזְכִּיר	הִזְכַּרְתְּ	הִזְכַּרְתָּ	הִזְכַּרְתִּי	ז־כ־ר	remind, make remember
הֶחֱיוּ	הֶחֱיִיתֶן	הֶחֱיִיתֶם	הֶחֱיִינוּ	הֶחֶיְתָה	הֶחֱיָה	הֶחֱיִית	הֶחֱיִיתָ	הֶחֱיִיתִי	ח־י־ה	keep alive

הֵם\הֵן **they *m/f***	אַתֶּן **you *f pl***	אַתֶּם **you *m pl***	אֲנַחְנוּ **we**	הִיא **she**	הוּא **he**	אַתְּ **you *f***	אַתָּה **you *m***	אֲנִי **I**	**Root**	**Meaning**
הוֹדִיעוּ	הוֹדַעְתֶּן	הוֹדַעְתֶּם	הוֹדַעְנוּ	הוֹדִיעָה	הוֹדִיעַ	הוֹדַעַתְּ	הוֹדַעְתָּ	הוֹדַעְתִּי	י־ד־ע	make known, announce
הוֹצִיאוּ	הוֹצֵאתֶן	הוֹצֵאתֶם	הוֹצֵאנוּ	הוֹצִיאָה	הוֹצִיא	הוֹצֵאת	הוֹצֵאתָ	הוֹצֵאתִי	י־צ־א	bring out, take out
הוֹשִׁיבוּ	הוֹשַׁבְתֶּן	הוֹשַׁבְתֶּם	הוֹשַׁבְנוּ	הוֹשִׁיבָה	הוֹשִׁיב	הוֹשַׁבְתְּ	הוֹשַׁבְתָּ	הוֹשַׁבְתִּי	י־ש־ב	cause to sit, dwell, seat
הֵמִיתוּ	הֲמַתֶּן	הֲמַתֶּם	הֲמַתְנוּ	הֵמִיתָה	הֵמִית	הֲמַתְּ	הֲמַתָּ	הֲמַתִּי	מ־ו־ת	kill, put to death
הִמְלִיכוּ	הִמְלַכְתֶּן	הִמְלַכְתֶּם	הִמְלַכְנוּ	הִמְלִיכָה	הִמְלִיךְ	הִמְלַכְתְּ	הִמְלַכְתָּ	הִמְלַכְתִּי	מ־ל־ך	make king or queen, crown
הֵנִיחוּ	הֲנַחְתֶּן	הֲנַחְתֶּם	הֲנַחְנוּ	הֵנִיחָה	הֵנִיחַ	הֲנַחַתְּ	הֲנַחְתָּ	הֲנַחְתִּי	נ־ו־ח	pacify, calm, cause to rest
הֶעֱבִידוּ	הֶעֱבַדְתֶּן	הֶעֱבַדְתֶּם	הֶעֱבַדְנוּ	הֶעֱבִידָה	הֶעֱבִיד	הֶעֱבַדְתְּ	הֶעֱבַדְתָּ	הֶעֱבַדְתִּי	ע־ב־ד	put to work, employ
הֶעֱבִירוּ	הֶעֱבַרְתֶּן	הֶעֱבַרְתֶּם	הֶעֱבַרְנוּ	הֶעֱבִירָה	הֶעֱבִיר	הֶעֱבַרְתְּ	הֶעֱבַרְתָּ	הֶעֱבַרְתִּי	ע־ב־ר	cause to pass, bring across
הֶעֱלוּ	הֶעֱלִיתֶן	הֶעֱלִיתֶם	הֶעֱלִינוּ	הֶעֶלְתָה	הֶעֱלָה	הֶעֱלִית	הֶעֱלִיתָ	הֶעֱלִיתִי	ע־ל־ה	raise, cause to ascend
הֶעֱמִידוּ	הֶעֱמַדְתֶּן	הֶעֱמַדְתֶּם	הֶעֱמַדְנוּ	הֶעֱמִידָה	הֶעֱמִיד	הֶעֱמַדְתְּ	הֶעֱמַדְתָּ	הֶעֱמַדְתִּי	ע־מ־ד	establish, make stand
הֶרְאוּ	הֶרְאֵיתֶן	הֶרְאֵיתֶם	הֶרְאֵינוּ	הֶרְאֲתָה	הֶרְאָה	הֶרְאֵית	הֶרְאֵיתָ	הֶרְאֵיתִי	ר־א־ה	cause to see,show
הִשְׁמִיעוּ	הִשְׁמַעְתֶּן	הִשְׁמַעְתֶּם	הִשְׁמַעְנוּ	הִשְׁמִיעָה	הִשְׁמִיעַ	הִשְׁמַעַתְּ	הִשְׁמַעְתָּ	הִשְׁמַעְתִּי	ש־מ־ע	make heard, proclaim

הִפְעִיל Participle

Feminine Plural	Masculine Plural	Feminine Singular	Masculine Singular	Root	Meaning
מַאֲכִילוֹת	מַאֲכִילִים	מַאֲכִילָה	מַאֲכִיל	א־כ־ל	cause to eat, feed
מַאֲמִינוֹת	מַאֲמִינִים	מַאֲמִינָה	מַאֲמִין	א־מ־ן	trust, believe
מְבִיאוֹת	מְבִיאִים	מְבִיאָה	מֵבִיא	ב־ו־א	cause to come, bring
מוֹלִיכוֹת	מוֹלִיכִים	מוֹלִיכָה	מוֹלִיךְ	ה־ל־ך	cause to go, lead, conduct
מַזְכִּירוֹת	מַזְכִּירִים	מַזְכִּירָה	מַזְכִּיר	ז־כ־ר	remind, make remember
מַחֲיוֹת	מַחֲיִים	מַחֲיָה	מַחֲיֶה	ח־י־ה	keep alive
מוֹדִיעוֹת	מוֹדִיעִים	מוֹדִיעָה	מוֹדִיעַ	י־ד־ע	make known, announce
מוֹצִיאוֹת	מוֹצִיאִים	מוֹצִיאָה	מוֹצִיא	י־צ־א	bring out, take out
מוֹשִׁיבוֹת	מוֹשִׁיבִים	מוֹשִׁיבָה	מוֹשִׁיב	י־שׁ־ב	cause to sit, dwell, seat
מְמִיתוֹת	מְמִיתִים	מְמִיתָה	מֵמִית	מ־ו־ת	kill, put to death
מַמְלִיכוֹת	מַמְלִיכִים	מַמְלִיכָה	מַמְלִיךְ	מ־ל־ך	make king or queen, crown
מְנִיחוֹת	מְנִיחִים	מְנִיחָה	מֵנִיחַ	נ־ו־ח	pacify, calm, cause to rest
מַעֲבִידוֹת	מַעֲבִידִים	מַעֲבִידָה	מַעֲבִיד	ע־ב־ד	put to work, employ
מַעֲבִירוֹת	מַעֲבִירִים	מַעֲבִירָה	מַעֲבִיר	ע־ב־ר	cause to pass, bring across
מַעֲלוֹת	מַעֲלִים	מַעֲלָה	מַעֲלֶה	ע־ל־ה	raise, cause to ascend
מַעֲמִידוֹת	מַעֲמִידִים	מַעֲמִידָה	מַעֲמִיד	ע־מ־ד	establish, make stand
מַרְאוֹת	מַרְאִים	מַרְאָה	מַרְאֶה	ר־א־ה	cause to see, show
מַשְׁמִיעוֹת	מַשְׁמִיעִים	מַשְׁמִיעָה	מַשְׁמִיעַ	שׁ־מ־ע	make heard, proclaim

הִפְעִיל Imperfect

הֵם they m/f	אַתֶּן, הֵן you, they f pl	אַתֶּם you m pl	אֲנַחְנוּ we	הִיא she	הוּא he	אַתְּ you f	אַתָּה you m	אֲנִי I	Root	Meaning
יַאֲכִילוּ	תַּאֲכֵלְנָה	תַּאֲכִילוּ	נַאֲכִיל	תַּאֲכִיל	יַאֲכִיל	תַּאֲכִילִי	תַּאֲכִיל	אַאֲכִיל	א־כ־ל	cause to eat, feed
יַאֲמִינוּ	תַּאֲמֵנָּה	תַּאֲמִינוּ	נַאֲמִין	תַּאֲמִין	יַאֲמִין	תַּאֲמִינִי	תַּאֲמִין	אַאֲמִין	א־מ־ן	trust, believe
יָבִיאוּ	תָּבֶאנָה	תָּבִיאוּ	נָבִיא	תָּבִיא	יָבִיא	תָּבִיאִי	תָּבִיא	אָבִיא	ב־ו־א	cause to come, bring
יוֹלִיכוּ	תּוֹלֵכְנָה	תּוֹלִיכוּ	נוֹלִיךְ	תּוֹלִיךְ	יוֹלִיךְ	תּוֹלִיכִי	תּוֹלִיךְ	אוֹלִיךְ	ה־ל־ך	cause to go, lead, conduct
יַזְכִּירוּ	תַּזְכֵּרְנָה	תַּזְכִּירוּ	נַזְכִּיר	תַּזְכִּיר	יַזְכִּיר	תַּזְכִּירִי	תַּזְכִּיר	אַזְכִּיר	ז־כ־ר	remind, make remember
יַחֲיוּ	תַּחֲיֶינָה	תַּחֲיוּ	נַחֲיֶה	תַּחֲיֶה	יַחֲיֶה	תַּחֲיִי	תַּחֲיֶה	אַחֲיֶה	ח־י־ה	keep alive
יוֹדִיעוּ	תּוֹדַעְנָה	תּוֹדִיעוּ	נוֹדִיעַ	תּוֹדִיעַ	יוֹדִיעַ	תּוֹדִיעִי	תּוֹדִיעַ	אוֹדִיעַ	י־ד־ע	make known, announce
יוֹצִיאוּ	תּוֹצֶאנָה	תּוֹצִיאוּ	נוֹצִיא	תּוֹצִיא	יוֹצִיא	תּוֹצִיאִי	תּוֹצִיא	אוֹצִיא	י־צ־א	bring out, take out
יוֹשִׁיבוּ	תּוֹשֵׁבְנָה	תּוֹשִׁיבוּ	נוֹשִׁיב	תּוֹשִׁיב	יוֹשִׁיב	תּוֹשִׁיבִי	תּוֹשִׁיב	אוֹשִׁיב	י־ש־ב	cause to sit, dwell, seat
יָמִיתוּ	תָּמֵתְנָה	תָּמִיתוּ	נָמִית	תָּמִית	יָמִית	תָּמִיתִי	תָּמִית	אָמִית	מ־ו־ת	kill, put to death
יַמְלִיכוּ	תַּמְלֵכְנָה	תַּמְלִיכוּ	נַמְלִיךְ	תַּמְלִיךְ	יַמְלִיךְ	תַּמְלִיכִי	תַּמְלִיךְ	אַמְלִיךְ	מ־ל־ך	make king or queen, crown
יָנִיחוּ	תָּנַחְנָה	תָּנִיחוּ	נָנִיחַ	תָּנִיחַ	יָנִיחַ	תָּנִיחִי	תָּנִיחַ	אָנִיחַ	נ־ו־ח	pacify, calm, cause to rest

הִפְעִיל **Imperfect** (continued)

הֵם **they m/f**	אַתֶּן, הֵן ***you, they f pl***	אַתֶּם **you *m pl***	אֲנַחְנוּ **we**	הִיא **she**	הוּא **he**	אַתְּ **you *f***	אַתָּה **you *m***	אֲנִי **I**	**Root**	**Meaning**
יַעֲבִידוּ	תַּעֲבֵדְנָה	תַּעֲבִידוּ	נַעֲבִיד	תַּעֲבִיד	יַעֲבִיד	תַּעֲבִידִי	תַּעֲבִיד	אַעֲבִיד	ע־ב־ד	put to work, employ
יַעֲבִירוּ	תַּעֲבֵרְנָה	תַּעֲבִירוּ	נַעֲבִיר	תַּעֲבִיר	יַעֲבִיר	תַּעֲבִירִי	תַּעֲבִיר	אַעֲבִיר	ע־ב־ר	cause to pass, bring across
יַעֲלוּ	תַּעֲלֶינָה	תַּעֲלוּ	נַעֲלֶה	תַּעֲלֶה	יַעֲלֶה	תַּעֲלִי	תַּעֲלֶה	אַעֲלֶה	ע־ל־ה	raise, cause to ascend
יַעֲמִידוּ	תַּעֲמֵדְנָה	תַּעֲמִידוּ	נַעֲמִיד	תַּעֲמִיד	יַעֲמִיד	תַּעֲמִידִי	תַּעֲמִיד	אַעֲמִיד	ע־מ־ד	establish, make stand
יַרְאוּ	תַּרְאֶינָה	תַּרְאוּ	נַרְאֶה	תַּרְאֶה	יַרְאֶה	תַּרְאִי	תַּרְאֶה	אַרְאֶה	ר־א־ה	cause to see, show
יַשְׁמִיעוּ	תַּשְׁמַעְנָה	תַּשְׁמִיעוּ	נַשְׁמִיעַ	תַּשְׁמִיעַ	יַשְׁמִיעַ	תַּשְׁמִיעִי	תַּשְׁמִיעַ	אַשְׁמִיעַ	ש־מ־ע	make heard, proclaim

Glossary

א

father, ancestor *m* (*A.I.E. Ch 5*) אָב, אָבוֹת
word pair forms אַב־ or אֲבִי־, אֲבוֹת־

stone *f* (*B.I.F.B. Ch 5*) אֶבֶן, אֲבָנִים
word pair forms אֶבֶן־, אַבְנֵי־

Abraham (*A.I.E. Ch 5*) אַבְרָהָם

lord, ruler *m* (*A.I.E. Ch 7*) אָדוֹן, אֲדוֹנִים
word pair forms אֲדוֹן־, אֲדוֹנֵי־

human being, man, humankind *m* (*B.I.F.B. Ch 3*) אָדָם

earth, ground, land *f* (*A.I.E. Ch 8*) אֲדָמָה, אֲדָמוֹת
word pair forms אַדְמַת־, אַדְמוֹת־

love (*A.I.E. Ch 6*) א־ה־ב (פָּעַל)

light *m* (*B.I.F.B. Ch 1*) אוֹר, אוֹרִים & אוֹרוֹת
word pair forms אוֹר־, אוֹרֵי־

then, at that time (*B.I.F.B. Ch 7*) אָז

brother *m* (*B.I.F.B. Ch 3*) אָח, אַחִים
word pair forms אַח־ or אֲחִי־, אֲחֵי־

one *m* (*plural:* a few, some) (*B.I.F.B. Ch 5*) אֶחָד, אֲחָדִים
word pair form אַחַד־

after, behind (*T.I.F.T. Ch 3*) אַחַר
with endings אַחֲרַי, אַחֲרֶיךָ, אַחֲרַיִךְ, אַחֲרָיו, אַחֲרֶיהָ, אַחֲרֵינוּ, אַחֲרֵיכֶם, אַחֲרֵיכֶן, אַחֲרֵיהֶם, אַחֲרֵיהֶן

other, another, different (*T.I.F.T. Ch 7*) אַחֵר, אַחֶרֶת, אֲחֵרִים, אֲחֵרוֹת

one *f* (*plural:* a few, some) (*B.I.F.B. Ch 5*) אַחַת, אֲחָדוֹת
word pair form אַחַת־

eat, consume (*A.I.E. Ch 2*) א־כ־ל (פָּעַל)

cause to eat, feed (*B.I.F.B. Ch 10*) (הִפְעִיל) –

there is/are not, there is/are none (*A.I.E. Ch 7*) אֵין
with endings אֵינִי or אֵינֶנִּי, אֵינְךָ, אֵינֵךְ, אֵינוֹ or אֵינֶנּוּ, אֵינָהּ or אֵינֶנָּה, אֵינֶנּוּ, אֵינְכֶם, אֵינְכֶן, אֵינָם, אֵינָן
[Note: The אֵין *forms with endings generally mean:* I (am) not, you (are) not, he/it (is) not, *etc.]*

man *m* (*B.I.F.B. Ch 3*) אִישׁ, אֲנָשִׁים
word pair forms אִישׁ־, אַנְשֵׁי־

no, not, don't (*T.I.F.T. Ch 5*) אַל

to, toward (*B.I.F.B. Ch 3*) אֶל
with endings אֵלַי, אֵלֶיךָ, אֵלַיִךְ, אֵלָיו, אֵלֶיהָ, אֵלֵינוּ, אֲלֵיכֶם, אֲלֵיכֶן, אֲלֵיהֶם, אֲלֵיהֶן

God *m* (*A.I.E. Ch 5*) אֵל
word pair form אֵל־

these (*T.I.F.T. Ch 1*) אֵלֶּה

God *m* (*A.I.E. Ch 4*) אֱלֹהִים
word pair form אֱלֹהֵי־

mother *f* (*A.I.E. Ch 5*) אֵם, אִמּוֹת & אִמָּהוֹת
word pair forms אֵם־, אִמּוֹת־

firmness, support, faithfulness, trust (*A.I.E. Ch 10*) א־מ־ן

trust, believe (*B.I.F.B. Ch 10*) (הִפְעִיל) –

say, utter, tell (*B.I.F.B. Ch 1*) א־מ־ר (פָּעַל)

truth *f* (*A.I.E. Ch 4*) אֱמֶת, אֲמִתּוֹת
word pair form אֱמֶת־

we (*A.I.E. Ch 2*) אֲנַחְנוּ, אָנוּ

I (*T.I.F.T. Ch 1*) אֲנִי

I (*T.I.F.T. Ch 1*) אָנֹכִי

earth, land *f* (*A.I.E. Ch 3*) אֶרֶץ, אֲרָצוֹת
word pair forms אֶרֶץ, אַרְצוֹת־

fire *f (T.I.F.T. Ch 3)* — אֵשׁ, אִשִּׁים

word pair forms — אֵשׁ־, אִשֵּׁי־

woman, wife *f (B.I.F.B. Ch 3)* — אִשָּׁה, נָשִׁים

word pair forms — אֵשֶׁת־, נְשֵׁי־

who, that, which *(A.I.E. Ch 8)* — אֲשֶׁר

definite direct object marker (untranslatable) (A.I.E. Ch 4); with *(preposition) (B.I.F.B. Ch 3)* — אֶת, אֵת

(untranslatable) with endings
אוֹתִי, אוֹתְךָ, אוֹתָךְ,
אוֹתוֹ, אוֹתָהּ, אוֹתָנוּ, אֶתְכֶם, אֶתְכֶן,
אוֹתָם, אוֹתָן

with *(preposition) with endings (B.I.F.B., Ch 3)* — אֶת, אֵת
אִתִּי, אִתְּךָ, אִתָּךְ, אִתּוֹ, אִתָּהּ,
אִתָּנוּ, אִתְּכֶם, אִתְּכֶן, אִתָּם, אִתָּן

you *m sg (A.I.E. Ch 1)* — אַתָּה

ב

with, in *(attached preposition) (A.I.E. Ch 6)* — בְּ־, בְ־

with endings בִּי, בְּךָ, בָּךְ, בּוֹ, בָּהּ,
בָּנוּ, בָּכֶם, בָּכֶן, בָּהֶם or בָּם, בָּהֶן

come *(T.I.F.T. Ch 3)* — ב־ו־א (פָּעַל)

cause to come, bring *(T.I.F.T. Ch 3)* — – (הִפְעִיל)

choose, select *(A.I.E. Ch 4)* — ב־ח־ר (פָּעַל)

between, among *(B.I.F.B. Ch 1)* — בֵּין

with endings בֵּינִי, בֵּינְךָ, בֵּינֵךְ, בֵּינוֹ,
בֵּינָהּ, בֵּינֵינוּ or בֵּינוֹתֵינוּ, בֵּינֵיכֶם,
בֵּינֵיכֶן, בֵּינֵיהֶם or בֵּינָם or בֵּינוֹתָם,
בֵּינֵיהֶן

house *m (A.I.E. Ch 6)* — בַּיִת, בָּתִּים

word pair forms — בֵּית־, בָּתֵּי־

son, child *m (A.I.E. Ch 3)* — בֵּן, בָּנִים

word pair forms — בֶּן־, בְּנֵי־

build *(B.I.F.B. Ch 5)* — ב־נ־ה

morning *m (B.I.F.B. Ch 1)* — בֹּקֶר, בְּקָרִים

word pair forms — בֹּקֶר־, בָּקְרֵי־

create *(A.I.E. Ch 3)* — ב־ר־א (פָּעַל)

Creation, in the beginning *(A.I.E. Ch 8)* — בְּרֵאשִׁית

bless *(A.I.E. Ch 1)* — ב־ר־ך (פִּעֵל)

blessed *(A.I.E. Ch 1)*
בָּרוּךְ, בְּרוּכָה, בְּרוּכִים, בְּרוּכוֹת

covenant *f (A.I.E. Ch 3)* — בְּרִית, בְּרִיתוֹת

word pair form — בְּרִית־

daughter *f (T.I.F.T. Ch 7)* — בַּת, בָּנוֹת

word pair forms — בַּת־, בְּנוֹת־

in the midst of, within *(T.I.F.T. Ch 3)* — בְּתוֹךְ

with endings בְּתוֹכִי, בְּתוֹכְךָ, בְּתוֹכֵךְ,
בְּתוֹכוֹ, בְּתוֹכָהּ, בְּתוֹכֵנוּ, בְּתוֹכְכֶם,
בְּתוֹכְכֶן, בְּתוֹכָם, בְּתוֹכָן

ג

mighty, valiant, courageous *adj (A.I.E. Ch 10)* — גִּבּוֹר, גִּבּוֹרָה,
גִּבּוֹרִים, גִּבּוֹרוֹת

strength, valor, might *f (A.I.E. Ch 10)* — גְּבוּרָה, גְּבוּרוֹת

word pair form — גְּבוּרַת־

big, great *adj (A.I.E. Ch 5)* — גָּדוֹל, גְּדוֹלָה,
גְּדוֹלִים, גְּדוֹלוֹת

nation, people *(A.I.E. Ch 8)* — גּוֹי, גּוֹיִם

word pair forms — גּוֹי־, גּוֹיֵי־

stranger, sojourner *m (in postbiblical Hebrew:* proselytes or converts to Judaism*) (T.I.F.T. Ch 5)* — גֵּר, גֵּרִים

word pair forms — גֵּר־, גֵּרֵי־

ד

speak, talk *(A.I.E. Ch 6)* — ד־ב־ר (פִּעֵל)

word, speech *(A.I.E. Ch 10) m;* thing *m (B.I.F.B. Ch 9)* — דָּבָר, דְּבָרִים

word pair forms דְּבַר־, דִּבְרֵי־

blood *m (B.I.F.B. Ch 3)* דָּם, דָּמִים

word pair forms דַּם־, דְּמֵי־

way, road, path *m* and *f (A.I.E. Ch 9)* דֶּרֶךְ, דְּרָכִים

word pair forms דֶּרֶךְ־, דַּרְכֵי־

ה

the *(attached prefix) (A.I.E. Ch 1)* הַ־, הָ־, הֶ־

toward *(attached ending) (T.I.F.T. Ch 1)* ◌ָה

her, it *(attached ending) f sg (A.I.E. Ch 9)* ־הָ

her, its, it *(attached ending) f sg (A.I.E. Ch 9)* ◌ָהּ

him, it *(attached ending) m sg (A.I.E. Ch 9)* ־הוּ

he, it *m (A.I.E. Ch 1)* הוּא

she, it *m (not included in vocabulary lists)* הִיא

be, exist *(B.I.F.B. Ch 1)* ה־י־ה (פָּעַל)

today *(T.I.F.T. Ch 9)* הַיּוֹם

walk, go *(B.I.F.B. Ch 9)* ה־ל־ך (פָּעַל)

cause to go, lead, bring, conduct *(B.I.F.B. Ch 10)* – (הִפְעִיל)

praise *(A.I.E. Ch 9)* ה־ל־ל (פִּעֵל)

Hallelujah, praise *Yah! (A.I.E. Ch 9)* הַלְלוּיָהּ

they *m (not included in vocabulary lists)* הֵם

their, them *(attached ending) (B.I.F.B. Ch 5)* ־הֶם

they *f (not included in vocabulary lists)* הֵן

behold, here [is]! *(B.I.F.B. Ch 9)* הִנֵּה

with endings הִנְנִי or הִנֵּנִי, הִנְּךָ or הִנֵּךְ, הִנָּךְ, הִנּוֹ or הִנֵּהוּ, הִנָּה or הִנֶּהָ, הִנֶּנּוּ or הִנֵּנוּ, הִנְּכֶם, הִנְּכֶן, הִנָּם, הִנָּן

mountain, mount *m (B.I.F.B. Ch 9)* הַר, הָרִים

word pair forms הַר־, הָרֵי־

ו

and *(attached prefix) (A.I.E. Ch 2)* וְ־, וּ־, וַ־, וָ־, וֵ־, וִ־

reversing vav – may or may not be translated וְ־, וּ־, וַ־, וָ *as "and".*

(attached prefix) (B.I.F.B. Ch 2) Generally וְ *or* וּ *when attached to perfect verbs, and* וַ *or* וָ *when attached to imperfect verbs.*

his, him, its, it *(attached ending) m sg (A.I.E. Ch 9)* ־וֹ

ז

this *f (T.I.F.T. Ch 1)* זֹאת

this *m (T.I.F.T. Ch 1)* זֶה

remember *(A.I.E. Ch 5)* ז־כ־ר (פָּעַל)

make remember, remind, mention *(B.I.F.B. Ch 10)* – (הִפְעִיל)

seed, offspring *m (B.I.F.B. Ch 7)* זֶרַע

word pair forms זֶרַע־

ח

sick, ill *m (A.I.E. Ch 9)* חוֹלֶה, חוֹלִים

word pair forms חוֹלֵה־, חוֹלֵי־

sick, ill *f (A.I.E. Ch 9)* חוֹלָה, חוֹלוֹת

word pair forms חוֹלַת־, חוֹלוֹת־

sin *m (T.I.F.T. Ch 5)* חֵטְא, חֲטָאִים

word pair forms חֵטְא־, חֲטָאֵי־

live, be alive *(bring to life) (A.I.E. Ch 8)* ח־י־ה

bring to life, give life *(A.I.E. Ch 10)* – (פִּעֵל)

keep alive *(B.I.F.B. Ch 10)* – (הִפְעִיל)

life *m (A.I.E. Ch 4)* חַיִּים

word pair form חַיֵּי־

leavened food *(not permitted during Passover) m (A.I.E. Ch 2)* חָמֵץ

fear, revere, be in awe (*T.I.F.T. Ch 1*) — י־ר־א (פָּעַל)

Jerusalem (*A.I.E. Ch 10*) — יְרוּשָׁלַיִם

there is, there are (*T.I.F.T. Ch 1*); being, substance, *or* existence — יֵשׁ

sit, settle, dwell (*B.I.F.B. Ch 5*) — י־שׁ־ב (פָּעַל)

cause to sit, seat, cause to dwell (*B.I.F.B. Ch 10*) — – (הִפְעִיל)

Israel *m* (*A.I.E. Ch 1*) — יִשְׂרָאֵל

כ

like, as (*attached preposition*) (*A.I.E. Ch 7*) — כְּ־, כַּ־

see כְּמוֹ *for other endings* — כָּכֶם, כָּהֶם

your, you (*attached ending*) *m sg* (*A.I.E. Ch 6*) — ־ךָ

as, when (*T.I.F.T. Ch 7*) — כַּאֲשֶׁר

honor, respect (*T.I.F.T. Ch 7*) — כ־ב־ד (פִּעֵל)

priest *m* (*T.I.F.T. Ch 3*) — כֹּהֵן, כֹּהֲנִים

word pair forms — כֹּהֵן־, כֹּהֲנֵי־

because, for; that (*T.I.F.T. Ch 3*) — כִּי

all, every (*A.I.E. Ch 8*) — כֹּל, כָּל

with endings כֻּלִּי, כֻּלְּךָ, כֻּלָּךְ or כֻּלֵּךְ, כֻּלּוֹ, כֻּלָּהּ, כֻּלָּנוּ, כֻּלְּכֶם, כֻּלְּכֶן, כֻּלָּם, כֻּלָּן

[Note: The כל *forms with endings generally mean:* "all of me", "all of it", *etc.]*

your, you (*attached ending*) *m pl* (*A.I.E. Ch 6*) — ־כֶם

like, as (*A.I.E. Ch 7*) — כְּמוֹ

with endings כָּמוֹנִי, כָּמוֹךָ or כָּמֹכָה, כָּמוֹךְ, כָּמוֹהוּ, כָּמוֹהָ, כָּמוֹנוּ, כְּמוֹכֶם, כְּמוֹכֶן, כְּמוֹהֶם, כְּמוֹהֶן

Canaan *m* (*B.I.F.B. Ch 7*) — כְּנַעַן

word pair form — חֲמֵץ־

Chanukah, dedication *f* (*A.I.E. Ch 8*) — חֲנֻכָּה

word pair form — חֲנֻכַּת־

kindness *m* (*A.I.E. Ch 5*) — חֶסֶד, חֲסָדִים

word pair forms — חֶסֶד־, חַסְדֵי־

darkness *m* (*B.I.F.B. Ch 1*) — חֹשֶׁךְ

word pair form — חֹשֶׁךְ־

ט

good *adj* (*A.I.E. Ch 5*) — טוֹב, טוֹבָה, טוֹבִים, טוֹבוֹת

י

my, me (*attached ending*) (*T.I.F.T. Ch 3*) — ◌ִי

my, me (*attached ending*) (*T.I.F.T. Ch 3*) — ◌ַי

hand *f* (*A.I.E. Ch 6*) — יָד, יָדַיִם

word pair forms — יַד־, יְדֵי־

know (*B.I.F.B. Ch 3*) — י־ד־ע (פָּעַל)

make known, inform, announce (*B.I.F.B. Ch 10*) — – (הִפְעִיל)

her, its, it (*attached ending*) *f sg* (*A.I.E. Ch 9*) — ◌ֶיהָ

Let [it] be, let [there] be (*from the root* ה־י־ה) (*B.I.F.B. Ch 2*) — יְהִי

his, him, its, it (*attached ending*) *m sg* (*A.I.E. Ch 9*) — ◌ָיו

day *m* (*A.I.E. Ch 3*) — יוֹם, יָמִים

word pair forms — יוֹם־, יְמֵי־

sea *m* (*T.I.F.T. Ch 1*) — יָם, יַמִּים

word pair forms — יָם־ or יַם־, יַמֵּי־

Jacob (*A.I.E. Ch 5*) — יַעֲקֹב

go out, come out (*A.I.E. Ch 10*) — י־צ־א (פָּעַל)

cause to go out, bring out (*B.I.F.B. Ch 10*) — – (הִפְעִיל)

Isaac (*A.I.E. Ch 5*) — יִצְחָק

ל

לְ־ to, for *(attached preposition) (A.I.E. Ch 8)*

with endings לִי, לְךָ, לָךְ, לוֹ, לָהּ,
לָנוּ, לָכֶם, לָכֶן, לָהֶם, לָהֶן

לֹא no, not *(B.I.F.B. Ch 3)*

לֵאָה Leah *(A.I.E. Ch 5)*

לֵאמֹר saying *(T.I.F.T. Ch 5)*

לֵב, לִבּוֹת heart *m (A.I.E. Ch 6)*

word pair forms לֵב־, לִבּוֹת־

לֵבָב, לְבָבוֹת heart *m (A.I.E. Ch 6)*

word pair forms לְבַב־, לִבְבוֹת־

לֶחֶם, לְחָמִים bread *m (A.I.E. Ch 3)*

word pair forms לֶחֶם־, לַחֲמֵי־

לַיְלָה, לֵילוֹת night *m (A.I.E. Ch 2)*

word pair forms לֵיל־, לֵילוֹת־

לְמַעַן in order to, so that, for the sake of *(T.I.F.T. Ch 7)*

with endings לְמַעֲנִי, לְמַעַנְךָ, לְמַעֲנֵךְ,
לְמַעֲנוֹ, לְמַעֲנָהּ, לְמַעֲנֵנוּ, לְמַעַנְכֶם,
לְמַעַנְכֶן, לְמַעֲנָם, לְמַעֲנָן

לְעוֹלָם וָעֶד forever and ever *(A.I.E. Ch 1)*

לִפְנֵי before *(T.I.F.T. Ch 9)*

with endings לְפָנַי, לְפָנֶיךָ, לְפָנַיִךְ,
לְפָנָיו, לְפָנֶיהָ, לְפָנֵינוּ, לִפְנֵיכֶם,
לִפְנֵיכֶן, לִפְנֵיהֶם, לִפְנֵיהֶן

ל־ק־ח (פָּעַל) take *(T.I.F.T. Ch 1)*

מ

מִ־, מֵ־ from, than *(attached preposition) (A.I.E. Ch 10)*

with endings – see מִן

ָם their, them *(attached ending) (B.I.F.B. Ch 5)*

מִדְבָּר, מִדְבָּרִים & מִדְבָּרוֹת wilderness, desert *m (T.I.F.T. Ch 3)*

word pair forms מִדְבַּר־, מִדְבְּרֵי־ or מִדְבְּרוֹת־

מוֹשִׁיעַ, מוֹשִׁיעִים savior, deliverer *m (A.I.E. Ch 7)*

word pair forms מוֹשִׁיעַ־, מוֹשִׁיעֵי־

מ־ו־ת (פָּעַל) die *(T.I.F.T. Ch 9)*

– (הִפְעִיל) cause to die, kill, put to death *(T.I.F.T. Ch 9)*

מָוֶת death *m (T.I.F.T. Ch 9)*

word pair form מוֹת־

מְזוּזָה, מְזוּזוֹת doorpost, mezuzah *f (A.I.E. Ch 6)*

word pair forms מְזוּזַת־, מְזוּזוֹת־

מִי who *(A.I.E. Ch 7)*

מַיִם water, waters *m, pl (B.I.F.B. Ch 1)*

word pair form מֵי־ or מֵימֵי־

מַלְאָךְ, מַלְאָכִים angel, messenger *m (A.I.E. Ch 6)*

word pair forms מַלְאַךְ־, מַלְאֲכֵי־

מְלָאכָה, מְלָאכוֹת work, labor, occupation *f (T.I.F.T. Ch 7)*

word pair forms מְלֶאכֶת־, מַלְאֲכוֹת־

מ־ל־ך (פָּעַל) rule, reign *(A.I.E. Ch 2)*

– (הִפְעִיל) make king or queen, crown *(B.I.F.B. Ch 10)*

מֶלֶךְ, מְלָכִים sovereign, king, ruler *m (A.I.E. Ch 2)*

word pair forms מֶלֶךְ־, מַלְכֵי־

מִן from, than *(A.I.E. Ch 10)*

with endings מִמֶּנִּי, מִמְּךָ, מִמֵּךְ,
מִמֶּנּוּ, מִמֶּנָּה, מִמֶּנּוּ, מִכֶּם, מִכֶּן,
מֵהֶם or מִנְהֶם or מֵהֵמָּה,
מֵהֶן or מֵהֵנָּה

מַעֲשֶׂה, מַעֲשִׂים deed, act, work *f (A.I.E. Ch 7)*

מַעֲשֵׂה־, מַעֲשֵׂי־ — *word pair forms*

מַצָּה, מַצּוֹת — matzah, unleavened bread *f (A.I.E. Ch 2)*

מַצַּת־, מַצּוֹת־ — *word pair forms*

מִצְוָה, מִצְוֹת — mitzvah, commandment *f (A.I.E. Ch 2)*

מִצְוַת־, מִצְוֹת־ — *word pair forms*

מִצְרַיִם — Egypt *(A.I.E. Ch 10)*

מָקוֹם, מְקוֹמוֹת — place *m (B.I.F.B. Ch 7)*

– הַמָּקוֹם — *literally:* the place, *a rabbinic term for God: the Omnipresent*

מְקוֹם־, מְקוֹמוֹת־ — *word pair forms*

מָרוֹר, מְרוֹרִים — bitter herb *m (A.I.E. Ch 2)*

מְרוֹר־, מְרוֹרֵי־ — *word pair forms*

מֹשֶׁה — Moses *(A.I.E. Ch 4)*

מִשְׁפָּחָה, מִשְׁפָּחוֹת — family *f (A.I.E. Ch 8)*

מִשְׁפַּחַת־, מִשְׁפְּחוֹת־ — *word pair forms*

מִשְׁפָּט, מִשְׁפָּטִים — justice, judgment, law *m (T.I.F.T. Ch 5)*

מִשְׁפַּט־, מִשְׁפְּטֵי־ — *word pair forms*

מִתּוֹךְ — from the midst of, out of, from among *(T.I.F.T. Ch 3)*

word pair forms — מִתּוֹכִי, מִתּוֹכְךָ, מִתּוֹכֵךְ, מִתּוֹכוֹ, מִתּוֹכָהּ, מִתּוֹכֵנוּ, מִתּוֹכְכֶם, מִתּוֹכְכֶן, מִתּוֹכָם, מִתּוֹכָן

נ

נָבִיא, נְבִיאִים — prophet *m (A.I.E. Ch 4)*

נְבִיא־, נְבִיאֵי־ — *word pair forms*

־נוּ — our, us (*on perfect verbs:* we) *(attached ending) (A.I.E. Ch 7; T.I.F.T. Ch 10)*

נ־ו־ח (פָּעַל) — rest *(T.I.F.T. Ch 7)*

– (הִפְעִיל) — cause to rest, pacify, calm *(T.I.F.T. Ch 7)*

־נִי — me *(attached ending) (T.I.F.T. Ch 3)*

נַעַר, נְעָרִים — lad, youth, young man *m (B.I.F.B. Ch 9)*

נַעַר־, נַעֲרֵי־ — *word pair forms*

נֶפֶשׁ, נְפָשׁוֹת — soul, mind, breath *f (A.I.E. Ch 6)*

נֶפֶשׁ־, נַפְשׁוֹת־ — *word pair forms*

נֵר, נֵרוֹת — light, candle, lamp *m (A.I.E. Ch 8)*

נֵר־, נֵרוֹת־ — *word pair forms*

נ־שׂ־א (פָּעַל) — lift, bear, carry *(T.I.F.T. Ch 5)*

נָשִׁים — women, wives *f (B.I.F.B. Ch 3) (plural of* אִשָּׁה*)*

נְשֵׁי־ — *word pair form*

נְשָׁמָה, נְשָׁמוֹת — living being, soul, breath, breathing *f (A.I.E. Ch 9)*

נִשְׁמַת־, נִשְׁמוֹת־ — *word pair forms*

נ־ת־ן (פָּעַל) — give, grant, permit *(A.I.E. Ch 4)*

ע

ע־ב־ד (פָּעַל) — work, serve *(B.I.F.B. Ch 3)*

– (הִפְעִיל) — put to work, employ *(B.I.F.B. Ch 10)*

עֶבֶד, עֲבָדִים — slave, bondsman, servant *m (A.I.E. Ch 10)*

עֶבֶד־, עַבְדֵי־ — *word pair forms*

ע־ב־ר (פָּעַל) — pass (over, through, by), cross *(T.I.F.T. Ch 9)*

– (הִפְעִיל) — cause to pass (over, through, by), bring across, transport *(T.I.F.T. Ch 9)*

עַד — until, unto, as far as *(B.I.F.B. Ch 7)*

with endings — עָדַי, עָדֶיךָ, עָדַיִךְ, עָדָיו, עָדֶיהָ, עָדֵינוּ, עֲדֵיכֶם, עֲדֵיכֶן, עֲדֵיהֶם, עֲדֵיהֶן

עֵדָה, עֵדוֹת — congregation, assembly, community *f (T.I.F.T. Ch 5)*

עֲדַת־, עֵדוֹת־ — *word pair forms*

עוֹלָם, עוֹלָמִים — universe, eternity, world *m*

& עוֹלָמוֹת *(A.I.E. Ch 1)*

word pair forms עוֹלַם־, עוֹלְמֵי־ or עוֹלְמוֹת־

help *(A.I.E. Ch 5)* ע־ז־ר (פָּעַל)

eye *f (B.I.F.B. Ch 9)* עַיִן, עֵינַיִם

word pair forms עֵין־, עֵינֵי־

city *f (B.I.F.B. Ch 5)* עִיר, עָרִי

word pair forms עִיר־, עָרֵי־

on, about *(A.I.E. Ch 8)* עַל

with endings עָלַי, עָלֶיךָ, עָלַיִךְ, עָלָיו, עָלֶיהָ, עָלֵינוּ, עֲלֵיכֶם, עֲלֵיכֶן, עֲלֵיהֶם, עֲלֵיהֶן

go up, ascend *(B.I.F.B. Ch 9)* ע־ל־ה (פָּעַל)

cause to ascend, bring up, raise *(B.I.F.B. Ch 10)* – (הִפְעִיל)

with *(B.I.F.B. Ch 9)* עִם

with endings עִמִּי or עִמָּדִי, עִמְּךָ, עִמָּךְ, עִמּוֹ, עִמָּהּ, עִמָּנוּ, עִמָּכֶם, עִמָּכֶן, עִמָּם or עִמָּהֶם, עִמָּן or עִמָּהֶן

people, nation *m (A.I.E. Ch 4)* עַם, עַמִּים

word pair forms עַם־, עַמֵּי־

stand *(T.I.F.T. Ch 5)* ע־מ־ד (פָּעַל)

cause to stand, erect, set up, establish *(T.I.F.T. Ch 5)* – (הִפְעִיל)

tree, wood *m (B.I.F.B. Ch 9)* עֵץ, עֵצִים

word pair forms עֵץ־, עֲצֵי־

evening *m (B.I.F.B. Ch 1)* עֶרֶב, עֲרָבִים

word pair forms עֶרֶב־, עַרְבֵי־

make, do, act *(A.I.E. Ch 7)* ע־שׂ־ה (פָּעַל)

פ

face, faces, surface *m* and *f, pl (B.I.F.B. Ch 1)* פָּנִים

word pair form פְּנֵי־

fruit *m (A.I.E. Ch 3)* פְּרִי, פֵּרוֹת

word pair forms פְּרִי־, פֵּרוֹת־

צ

righteousness, justice *m (A.I.E. Ch 4)* צֶדֶק

word pair form צֶדֶק־

righteousness, justice, *tzedakah f (A.I.E. Ch 7)* צְדָקָה, צְדָקוֹת

word pair forms צִדְקַת־, צִדְקוֹת־

command, order *(A.I.E. Ch 8)* צ־ו־ה (פִּעֵל)

Zion *(A.I.E. Ch 10)* צִיּוֹן

ק

holy, sacred, set apart *(A.I.E. Ch 7)* ק־ד־שׁ (פִּעֵל)

make holy *(A.I.E. Ch 10)* – (פִּעֵל)

holy, sacred *adj (A.I.E. Ch 6)* קָדוֹשׁ, קְדוֹשָׁה, קְדוֹשִׁים, קְדוֹשׁוֹת

holiness, sanctity *m (A.I.E. Ch 7)* קֹדֶשׁ, קֳדָשִׁים

word pair forms קֹדֶשׁ־, קָדְשֵׁי־

sound, voice *m (B.I.F.B. Ch 3)* קוֹל, קוֹלוֹת

word pair forms קוֹל־, קוֹלוֹת־

near, close *(T.I.F.T. Ch 9)* קָרוֹב, קְרוֹבָה, קְרוֹבִים, קְרוֹבוֹת

ר

see *(T.I.F.T. Ch 3)* ר־א־ה (פָּעַל)

cause to see, show *(T.I.F.T. Ch 3)* – (הִפְעִיל)

head, top, beginning *m (B.I.F.B. Ch 5)* רֹאשׁ, רָאשִׁים

word pair forms רֹאשׁ־, רָאשֵׁי־

numerous, many, great *adj (A.I.E. Ch 10)* רַב, רַבָּה, רַבִּים, רַבּוֹת

Rebekah *(A.I.E. Ch 5)* רִבְקָה

spirit, wind *m* and *f (B.I.F.B. Ch 1)* רוּחַ, רוּחוֹת

hear, listen, obey *(A.I.E. Ch 1)* שׁ־מ־ע (פָּעַל)

make heard, proclaim *(B.I.F.B. Ch 10)* – (הִפְעִיל)

guard, keep, preserve *(A.I.E. Ch 3)* שׁ־מ־ר (פָּעַל)

year *f (B.I.F.B. Ch 7)* שָׁנָה, שָׁנִים

literally: a son of…years; *an idiom for* …years old בֶּן...שָׁנִים

literally: a daughter of…years; *an idiom for* …years old בַּת...שָׁנִים

word pair forms שְׁנַת־, שְׁנֵי or שְׁנוֹת

gate *m (T.I.F.T. Ch 7)* שַׁעַר, שְׁעָרִים

word pair forms שַׁעַר־, שַׁעֲרֵי־

Sarah *(A.I.E. Ch 5)* שָׂרָה

ת

midst of, middle of *(T.I.F.T. Ch 3)* תּוֹךְ

with endings תּוֹכִי, תּוֹכְךָ, תּוֹכֵךְ, תּוֹכוֹ, תּוֹכָהּ, תּוֹכֵנוּ, תּוֹכְכֶם, תּוֹכְכֶן, תּוֹכָם, תּוֹכָן

Torah, teaching, law *f* תּוֹרָה, תּוֹרוֹת

word pair forms תּוֹרַת־, תּוֹרוֹת־ *(A.I.E. Ch 4)*

Key

A.I.E. = appears in *Aleph Isn't Enough*
B.I.F.B. = appears in *Bet Is for B'reishit*
T.I.F.T. = appears in *Tav Is for Torah*

word pair forms רוּחַ־, רוּחוֹת־

Rachel *(A.I.E. Ch 5)* רָחֵל

compassion, mercy *m* רַחֲמִים

word pair form (A.I.E. Ch 9) רַחֲמֵי־

evil *m (T.I.F.T. Ch 9)* רַע

word pair form רַע־

evil, bad, wicked *adj (T.I.F.T. Ch 9)* רַע, רָעָה, רָעִים, רָעוֹת

friend, companion, fellow, neighbor *m (B.I.F.B. Ch 5)* רֵעַ, רֵעִים

one…another [*Lit:* a man…his fellow] אִישׁ...רֵעֵהוּ

word pair forms רֵעַ־, רֵעֵי־

heal, cure *(A.I.E. Ch 9)* ר־פ־א (פָּעַל)

healing *f (A.I.E. Ch 9)* רְפוּאָה, רְפוּאוֹת

word pair forms רְפוּאַת־, רְפוּאוֹת־

שׁ

who, that, which *(attached prefix) (A.I.E. Ch 8)* שֶׁ־

Shabbat, Sabbath *f (A.I.E. Ch 3)* שַׁבָּת, שַׁבָּתוֹת

word pair forms שַׁבַּת־, שַׁבְּתוֹת־

shofar, ram's horn, horn *m (A.I.E. Ch 9)* שׁוֹפָר, שׁוֹפְרוֹת

word pair forms שׁוֹפַר־, שׁוֹפְרוֹת־

peace *m (A.I.E. Ch 6)* שָׁלוֹם, שְׁלוֹמִים & שְׁלוֹמוֹת

word pair forms שְׁלוֹם־, שְׁלוֹמֵי־ or שְׁלוֹמוֹת־

there *(B.I.F.B. Ch 5)* שָׁם

name *m (A.I.E. Ch 1)* שֵׁם, שֵׁמוֹת

word pair forms שֵׁם־ or שֶׁם־, שְׁמוֹת־

heavens, sky *m (A.I.E. Ch 3)* שָׁמַיִם

word pair form שְׁמֵי־

Notes

Notes